OCR

CRIME

& PUNISHMENT THROUGH TIME

The author would like to thank Alec Fisher for the story on pages 48–50.

The Schools History Project

Set up in 1972 to bring new life to history for students aged 13–16, the Schools History Project continues to play an innovatory role in secondary history education. From the start, SHP aimed to show how good history has an important contribution to make to the education of a young person. It does this by creating courses and materials which both respect the importance of up-to-date, well-researched history and provide enjoyable learning experiences for students.

Since 1978 the Project has been based at Trinity and All Saints University College Leeds. It continues to support, inspire and challenge teachers through the annual conference, regional courses and website: www.schoolshistoryproject.org.uk. The Project is also closely involved with government bodies and awarding bodies in the planning of courses for Key Stage 3, GCSE and A level.

Although every effort has been made to ensure that website addresses are correct at time of going to press, Hodder Education cannot be held responsible for the content of any website mentioned in this book. It is sometimes possible to find a relocated web page by typing in the address of the home page for a website in the URL window of your browser.

Hachette UK's policy is to use papers that are natural, renewable and recyclable products and made from wood grown in sustainable forests. The logging and manufacturing processes are expected to conform to the environmental regulations of the country of origin.

Orders: please contact Bookpoint Ltd, 130 Milton Park, Abingdon, Oxon OX14 4SB. Telephone: +44 (0)1235 827720. Fax: +44 (0)1235 400454. Lines are open 9.00a.m.–5.00p.m., Monday to Saturday, with a 24-hour message answering service. Visit our website at www.hoddereducation.co.uk.

© Richard McFahn, Christopher Culpin and Ian Dawson 2010
First published in 2010 by
Hodder Education,
an Hachette UK company
338 Euston Road
London NW1 3BH

Impression number	10 9 8 7 6 5 4 3 2 1
Year	2014 2013 2012 2011 2010

Typeset in 11/13 pt Palatino Light
Layouts by Lorraine Inglis Design
Artwork by Dylan Gibson, Barking Dog, Steve Smith, Peter Lubach and Richard Duszczak
Printed and bound in Italy

A catalogue record for this title is available from the British Library

ISBN 978 0 340 99135 0

OCR
CRIME
& PUNISHMENT THROUGH TIME

Richard McFahn

Christopher Culpin

with Ian Dawson

AN HACHETTE UK COMPANY

Contents

Key features of Smarter History –
Crime and Punishment through time

Before you start using this book here is a guide to help you get the most out of it.

Enquiries

The book is structured around a series of Enquiries, each one focusing on a key aspect of your GCSE course. Each Enquiry helps you understand a particular event, person or breakthrough and then links it to the broader history of crime and punishment.

Banners introduce each Enquiry so you know exactly what you are focusing on from the start.

Activities guide you through the material so you build up your knowledge and understanding of the key content of your GCSE course. They also link into the on-going Smarter Revision activities.

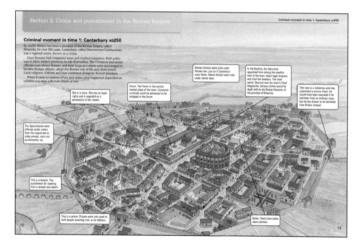

Crime and punishment moments in time

These pages give you an overview of the key features of crime and punishment at four important points in history – AD250, 650, 1732 and 1845.

How to ... sections give you clear advice on how to use each Smarter Revision strategy.

Smarter Revision

These pages help you prepare effectively for your examinations, showing you a variety of ways to build up your knowledge and understanding of the history of crime and punishment. You will be building up your revision material from the very beginning of your course – not waiting until you have completed it. See page 10 for more details on Smarter Revision pages.

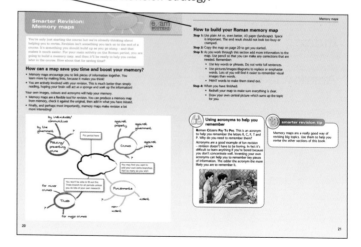

Meet the Examiner

These pages explain how to win high marks in your examinations. They show you how to:

- answer each type of question in your examinations
- identify exactly what a question is asking
- structure answers and develop your vocabulary to make full use of what you know.

Meet the Examiner pages cover both:

- Paper 1 Section A – Development Study
- Paper 2 – Historical Source Investigation.

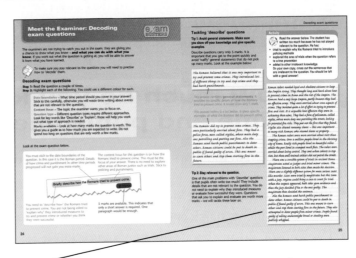

Sample answers help you identify what makes a good answer.

Dynamic Learning

Dynamic Learning provides an extensive range of supporting resources:

- Enquiries developing your knowledge and understanding of key topics within each period
- Thematic investigations helping you understand the development of major themes across time
- Extension activities to expand your knowledge.
- Decision-making activities to get you involved in the key issues.

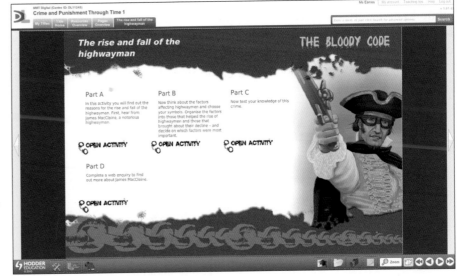

Section 1: The Big Story of crime and punishment through time – what do you think happened, and when?

1.1 How much do you know about crime and punishment today?

Crimes are often in the news. A particularly shocking crime can lead to heated discussions:

- Is crime becoming more violent?
- Are punishments harsh enough?
- Does prison do any good?
- Should people be locked away for longer?
- Should we bring back capital punishment?

People often voice their opinions without actually knowing the facts. Studying history can stop you being prejudiced. This course will help you come to an informed opinion about the nature of crime and punishment today. After all, the past has helped shape the present. The history of crime and punishment helps us see this very clearly.

So, what do you know about crime and punishment today? Fill in your own copy of this survey.

Crime survey

1 In the last ten years crime has:
- a) Risen dramatically ☐
- b) Stayed roughly the same ☐
- c) Fallen ☐

2 Violent crime is:
- a) 50% ☐
- b) 35% ☐
- c) 10% ☐
- d) 3% ☐

of all crime

3 Burglary is:
- a) Increasing dramatically ☐
- b) Increasing a little ☐
- c) Decreasing ☐
- d) Decreasing dramatically ☐

4 Car crime (theft of cars and possessions from cars) is:
- a) Increasing dramatically ☐
- b) Increasing a little ☐
- c) Decreasing ☐
- d) Decreasing dramatically ☐

5 How many fatal shootings were there in 2007?
- a) 1,564 ☐
- b) 523 ☐
- c) 59 ☐
- d) 2 ☐

6 Are men or women more likely to be attacked by a stranger?
- a) Men ☐
- b) Women ☐

7 Who is most likely to be mugged?
- a) Female pensioner ☐
- b) Male pensioner ☐
- c) Female under 29 ☐
- d) Male under 29 ☐

The authors of this book would be very surprised if you managed to get all of the answers to the crime survey correct. In fact we would be surprised if you got more than half of the answers correct. Most people think that crime is much worse than it actually is.

Activity

Why do you think most people think crime is much worse than it actually is?
Read the headlines below. They should give you a clue.

Another teenager stabbed to death

Boy shot in park highlights Britain's growing problem with gun crime

HEAD TEACHER STABBED TO DEATH OUTSIDE HIS SCHOOL

Gangs of criminals sell people's credit card details over the internet

One answer is the influence of the media. Stories about crime sell newspapers. People are interested in reading such stories; the more shocking the better. In fact people who read the tabloid newspapers are twice as likely to worry about crime compared to those who read the broadsheets.

1.2 Why are you studying the history of crime and punishment?

This course isn't trying to turn you into policemen or policewomen – and certainly not criminals! Its aim is to help you to get better at history and to enjoy finding out about the people who lived in the past. It is a Development Study, which means you will be studying a long period – 2,000 years. Pages 4–11 will help you to understand how this history course links together and how, by studying the history of crime and punishment, you can become a better historian.

1 It will improve your sense of chronology

You will increase your knowledge of some of the most important events in history, and understand better how they fit together, and why each period was important. You already know something about each of these periods from your earlier history courses. A Development Study helps you to see how all these periods fit together.

2 It will help you understand how people's lives have changed

The history of crime and punishment is an excellent case study. It's a detailed example of how people's everyday lives have changed. Two thousand years ago people's lives were very different from ours today – sometimes their attitudes seem very different too. Often, however, people's actions and their attitudes were surprisingly similar to our own – especially when it comes to crime.

3 It will help you explain *why* changes happened – and *why* they didn't happen

During this Development Study you won't just study what changed, you will try to work out why things changed or stayed the same. For example, you will see that mass media, such as newspapers, have been an important factor influencing people's attitudes to crime and punishment at different times. This is because newspapers exaggerate how much crime there is and make people more afraid of crime than they need to be.

On page 5 are a group of people you are going to meet regularly during the course. They are the reasons, the **factors**, which explain the changes and continuities in crime and punishment. They are:

- Government and Law Makers
- Beliefs and Ideas
- Religion
- Taxes
- Travel
- Media
- Towns
- Key Individuals
- Poverty and Wealth

There are nine factors. Sometimes two or more work together. Sometimes a factor doesn't apply at all. But you'll find them affecting what happens to crime and punishment right through the course so it's worth remembering them. You will be reminded to look for factors many times and whenever you see the 'factor wheel' opposite there will be an activity to focus on finding factors at work.

Activities

Think back to your KS3 history and what you learned about the features of the different periods shown on the timeline above. From what you already know:
1 Do you think the Middle Ages was a time of harsh punishments?
2 How might the Industrial Revolution have affected crime?
3 When do you think the first police force was introduced?
Keep your answers – you can check later to see if you were right.

Activities

Discuss the following:

4   Which of the factors do you think might cause an increase in crime?
5   Which of them might help reduce crime?
6   How might each of the factors lead to changes in punishments?

1.3 The Big Story – clues

The first thing you need for success in this course is an outline picture of the history of crime and punishment in your mind, and on paper. We'll start by getting you to think! Which period of history do you think each of these clues comes from?

The Big Story of capital punishment

Activity

The history of crime and punishment can be surprising. It can be very violent too – especially when you look at the history of punishments. In the past, humans seem to have been quite keen on killing each other as a form of punishment. This is known as capital punishment or execution.

1 Read clues A–H.
   a) What does each clue tell you about executions?
   b) What time period does each clue come from?
   c) Draw your own version of the timeline at the foot of these pages and pencil in each clue heading where you think it belongs.

Clue A: The Gunpowder Plot

A group of Catholics attempted to kill the king by blowing up Parliament. They were caught red handed, hanged in public, castrated, disembowelled and cut into quarters while they were still alive.

Clue B: William 'harries the north'

'Three years after I rightfully took control of this country, the people near York threatened my authority and tried to rebel. I treated them without mercy. My soldiers marched north and were ordered to kill everyone they could find, destroy the crops and burn the villages. The people of the north learned their lesson the hard way.'

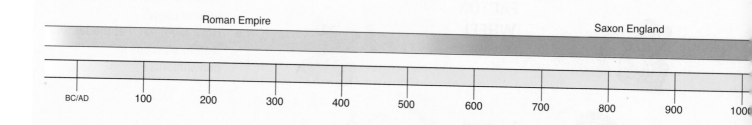

Roman Empire | Saxon England

BC/AD — 100 — 200 — 300 — 400 — 500 — 600 — 700 — 800 — 900 — 1000

Clue C: The Bloody Code

Crimes carrying the death penalty increased dramatically in this century.

'We wanted to stop crime. Harsh punishments deter people – don't they? Here are some of the crimes carrying the death penalty: stealing horses; sending threatening letters; pick-pocketing goods worth more than 5 shillings; stealing from a rabbit warren; being out at night with a blackened face …'

Clue D: Alfred the Great

The laws of Alfred the Great stated, 'If anyone plots against the king's life he forfeits his life and everything he owns.'

Clue F: The ending of the Bloody Code

Sir Robert Peel was the Home Secretary when nearly all capital crimes were abolished. Many politicians called for an end to this 'Bloody Code'. One wrote, ' … a man who has picked a pocket of a handkerchief worth thirteen pence is punished with the same severity as if he had murdered a whole family. [He is hanged.] None should be punished by death except in the cases of murder.'

Clue E: The last woman hanged

'It is immoral to hang Ruth Ellis for this crime. We are supposed to be a civilised nation. We own cars, listen to the radio and go to the cinema. Execution is far from civilised. It is degrading. The law must change.'

Clue G: Royal courts

The royal court record in Norfolk from this year stated, 'Hamon, son of John in the Corner, was taken for stealing at night a mare worth 10s, and for stealing one horse worth 13s 4d and for robbing Thomas le Nerve of goods worth 40s. He stands trial and is convicted. He is to be hanged.'

Clue H: The Cato Street Conspiracy

After the Napoleonic wars ended, the British government were still worried about revolution. People flooded to work in the new industrial cites where conditions were awful. A group of radicals attempted to assassinate the entire government. They were the last people to be beheaded in Britain.

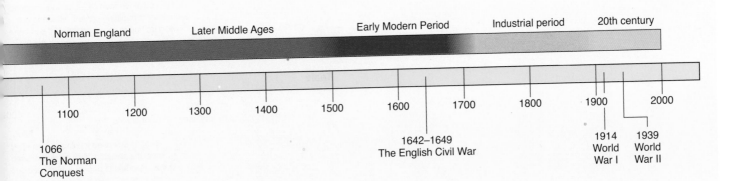

| Norman England | Later Middle Ages | Early Modern Period | Industrial period | 20th century |

1100   1200   1300   1400   1500   1600   1700   1800   1900   2000

1066
The Norman
Conquest

1642–1649
The English Civil War

1914
World
War I

1939
World
War II

The Big Picture of capital punishment through time

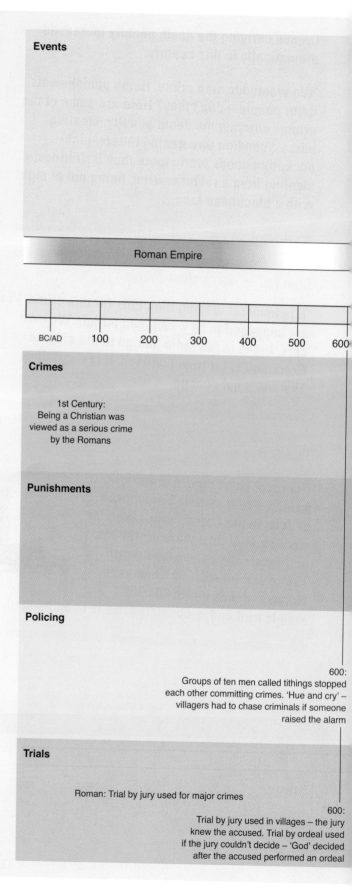

Events

Roman Empire

BC/AD   100   200   300   400   500   600

Crimes

1st Century:
Being a Christian was viewed as a serious crime by the Romans

Punishments

Policing

600:
Groups of ten men called tithings stopped each other committing crimes. 'Hue and cry' – villagers had to chase criminals if someone raised the alarm

Trials

Roman: Trial by jury used for major crimes

600:
Trial by jury used in villages – the jury knew the accused. Trial by ordeal used if the jury couldn't decide – 'God' decided after the accused performed an ordeal

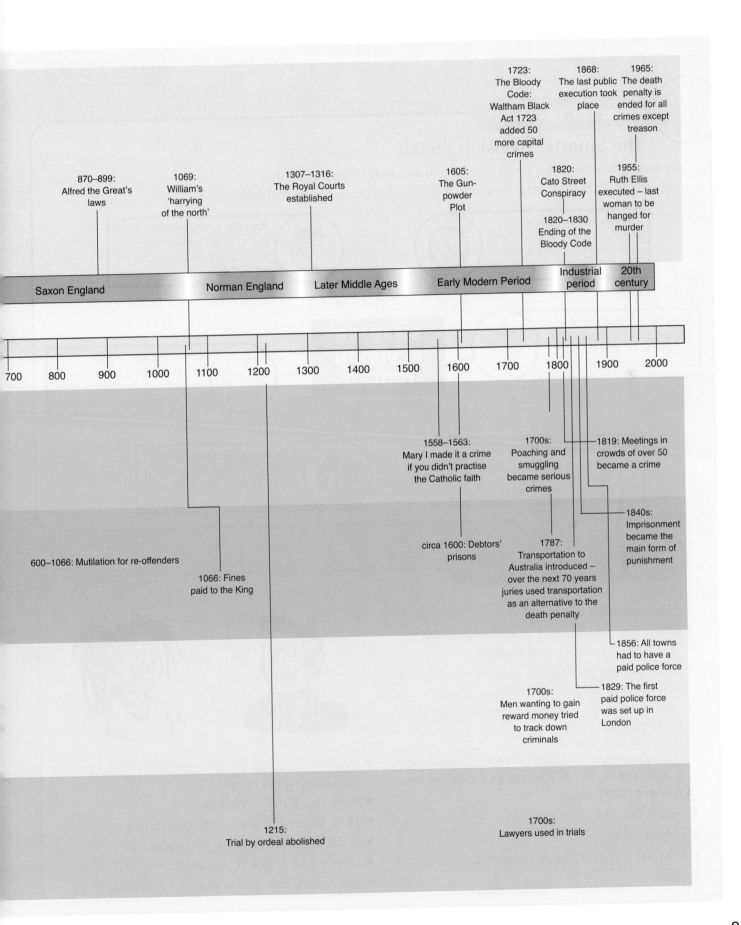

870–899: Alfred the Great's laws

1069: William's 'harrying of the north'

1307–1316: The Royal Courts established

1605: The Gun-powder Plot

1723: The Bloody Code: Waltham Black Act 1723 added 50 more capital crimes

1868: The last public execution took place

1965: The death penalty is ended for all crimes except treason

1820: Cato Street Conspiracy

1820–1830 Ending of the Bloody Code

1955: Ruth Ellis executed – last woman to be hanged for murder

Saxon England **Norman England** **Later Middle Ages** **Early Modern Period** **Industrial period** **20th century**

700   800   900   1000   1100   1200   1300   1400   1500   1600   1700   1800   1900   2000

1558–1563: Mary I made it a crime if you didn't practise the Catholic faith

1700s: Poaching and smuggling became serious crimes

1819: Meetings in crowds of over 50 became a crime

1840s: Imprisonment became the main form of punishment

600–1066: Mutilation for re-offenders

circa 1600: Debtors' prisons

1787: Transportation to Australia introduced – over the next 70 years juries used transportation as an alternative to the death penalty

1066: Fines paid to the King

1856: All towns had to have a paid police force

1700s: Men wanting to gain reward money tried to track down criminals

1829: The first paid police force was set up in London

1215: Trial by ordeal abolished

1700s: Lawyers used in trials

What are the best ways to prepare for your GCSE exams?

Good revision and planning will help you do well at GCSE. We will help you using the two important features below.

 smarter revision

The Smarter Revision toolkit

The toolkit will help you prepare your revision notes thoroughly and intelligently. Each tool helps you with a different aspect of your revision.

Factors wheel – helps you to hunt for factors that affect crime and punishment and record them. See page 5.

 Revision cards – help you to recall and organise information. See page 32, 38 and 42.

Timeline – helps you to see the big story of change and continuity in each theme. See page 11.

 Year

SMARTER REVISION TOOLKIT

 Concept map – helps you to link factors and so improve your explanation. See page 72.

Memory map – helps you remember the key developments in each period. See page 20.

 Punishment pendulum – helps you record the impact of key people. See page 100.

 meet the examiner

These pages will:

- advise you how to write good answers AND how to avoid writing bad answers
- show you sample answers and ask you to mark and improve them
- set you sample questions to improve your skills at writing good answers.

They will cover all the main types of question you will face in an OCR exam and explain how to answer them, e.g.:

- Briefly describe …
- Explain why …
- Why did they make more progress in … than … ?

- How did … affect the development of punishment over time?
- How much did … change … ?
- How far do you agree with this statement … ?
- What does Source X tell you about …
- How useful is this source for …
- Use the sources and your own knowledge to …

On pages 8–9 you saw the Big Picture of capital punishments – all in one timeline. Timelines like this are really helpful for following the story of crime and punishment across time so it's important to start early – NOW!

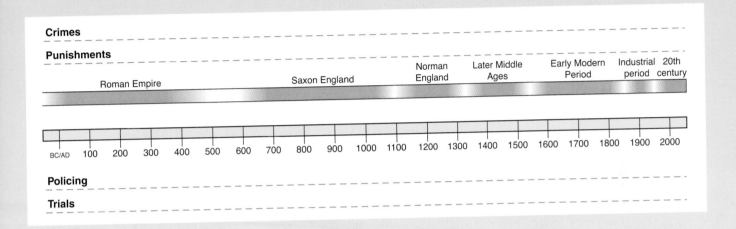

Crimes

Punishments

Roman Empire   Saxon England   Norman England   Later Middle Ages   Early Modern Period   Industrial period   20th century

BC/AD 100 200 300 400 500 600 700 800 900 1000 1100 1200 1300 1400 1500 1600 1700 1800 1900 2000

Policing

Trials

Activities

1 Look at the timeline above. On your own large copy, what would you pencil on this from your current knowledge? What crimes were committed at different times? What punishments were used? What forms of policing were there? What were trials like?

2 Work in groups of three and choose one of these four themes:
   a crimes
   b punishments
   c policing
   d trials.

3 Sections of this book start with a picture showing a 'criminal moment', indicating what crime, punishment, trials and policing were like at different dates. See pages 12–13, 26–27, 56–57 and 82–83.
   a From each picture, pick out the evidence about your theme and decide where you would place it on the timeline.

   b Use sticky notes to jot down the evidence and stick these on the timeline.

4 When you have completed your outline timeline you have one minute to explain it to the rest of the class. In your explanation you must use these words at least once:
   change   continuity   turning points.

5 Focus on the story of punishments that you have just heard, and think about the story of capital punishments. What reasons (listed below) help to explain the punishments used in the different time periods?
   a To deter criminals from committing crime.
   b To warn others from committing crime.
   c To compensate the victims.
   d To protect society.
   e To take revenge against the criminal.

Criminal moment in time 1: Canterbury AD250

By AD250, Britain had been a province of the Roman Empire, called Britannia, for over 200 years. Canterbury, called Durovernum Cantiacorum, was a regional centre, known as a *civitas*.

Once Romans had conquered areas and crushed resistance, their policy was to allow subject provinces to rule themselves. The Governor and senior officials were always Roman, and local kings and chiefs were encouraged to become Roman citizens, adopt the Roman way of life and share power. Local religions, customs and laws continued alongside Roman practices.

When it came to matters of law and order, what happened depended on whether you were a Roman citizen or not.

She is a slave. She has no legal rights and is regarded as a possession of her master.

Forum. The Forum is the central market place of the town. Convicted criminals could be sentenced to be whipped in the forum.

The *Speculatores* were officials under orders from the magistrate to make arrests, carry out punishments, etc.

This is a temple. The punishment for stealing from a temple was death.

This is a prison. Prisons were only used to hold people awaiting trial, or for debtors.

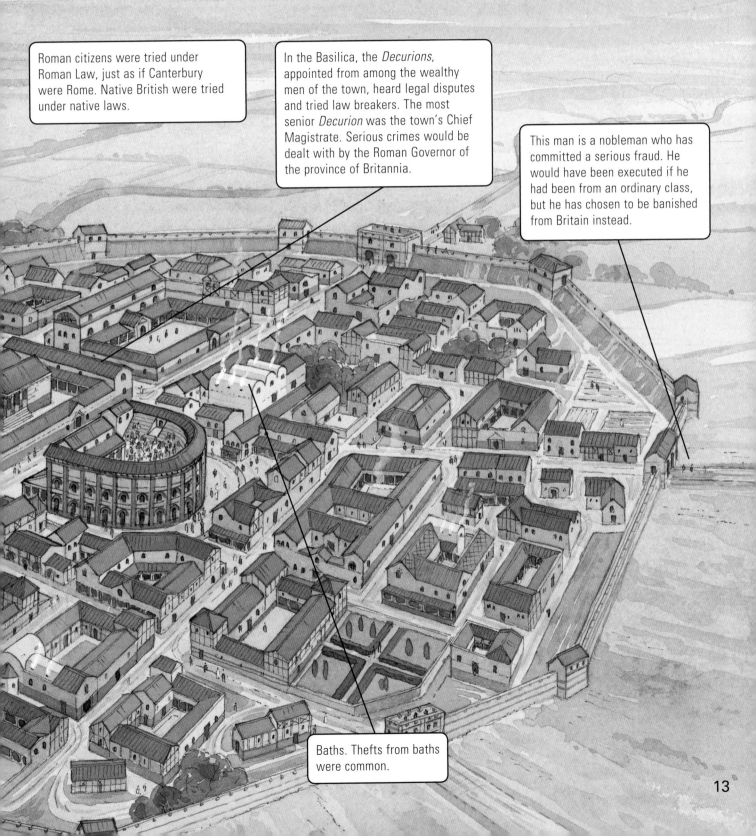

Roman citizens were tried under Roman Law, just as if Canterbury were Rome. Native British were tried under native laws.

In the Basilica, the *Decurions*, appointed from among the wealthy men of the town, heard legal disputes and tried law breakers. The most senior *Decurion* was the town's Chief Magistrate. Serious crimes would be dealt with by the Roman Governor of the province of Britannia.

This man is a nobleman who has committed a serious fraud. He would have been executed if he had been from an ordinary class, but he has chosen to be banished from Britain instead.

Baths. Thefts from baths were common.

2.1 How did the Romans try to prevent crime?

Think of the Romans and what images spring into your mind? Wealthy people wearing togas? Comfortable villas with central heating? An efficient army? Rational thinkers and planners who built well-organised towns and roads that ran straight for hundreds of miles? Although the Romans seem to have been way ahead of their time, some things in history don't change. People have always drunk alcohol and become rowdy. There have always been thieves and muggers. The Romans were no exception. The story you are going to look at is an example of this. It happened in 460BC – but it's a story that could happen today.

Murder in Rome

'I had a brother called Lucius. One evening we dined with a friend and afterwards, as night fell, we left for home. When we reached the Forum, Caeso and a band of young troublemakers began to follow us. At first they laughed at us and insulted us. Rich young men who have drunk too much enjoy insulting the poor.

'Lucius became angry and told Caeso what he thought of him. Caeso, who hated anyone standing up to him, ran up to Lucius and kicked him and beat him. I shouted for help and did all I could to defend my brother so Caeso turned on me, leaving Lucius lying dead in the street. He beat me until I too was motionless and speechless on the ground and he thought that I was dead.

'Caeso went away rejoicing, as if he had conquered an enemy in war. As for us, some passers-by picked us up, covered in blood though we were, and carried us home – my brother being dead and I half-dead.'

Activities

1 That story was told by Marcus Volscius in about the year 460BC. It was recorded by at least two Roman writers. The question is, 'what happened next?' Below are three alternative endings to the story. Think about what you already know about the Roman Empire. Was it a well-organised empire? Do you think that the Romans had good laws? What sorts of punishments do you think they used? Then decide which of the endings is the real one.

Ending A – Caeso was arrested by the Roman police. He was imprisoned until his trial. At the trial Volscius repeated his evidence and was questioned by Caeso. The jury decided that Caeso was guilty and he was executed by being thrown off the highest cliff in Rome.

Ending B – Caeso was taken by the police to the Emperor because he was a nobleman's son. The truth was decided by Caeso taking hold of a red-hot iron bar. His hand was bandaged. Three days later Caeso's hand was still badly blistered. He was guilty. The sentence was death but because he was a nobleman he was sent into exile many miles away from Rome.

Ending C – Volscius had to gather the evidence against Caeso himself. He took the evidence to a judge who decided that there should be a trial. Volscius and Caeso hired lawyers and the case was heard by a jury of Roman citizens who decided both whether Caeso was guilty and what the punishment should be. He was found guilty. The sentence was death but because he was a nobleman he was sent into exile many miles away from Rome.

2   On pages 16–17 you can find out more about crime, punishment and policing in ancient Rome. Match the statements 1–15 with the features shown in the picture on pages 16–17.

Statements

1   Anyone who deliberately burned down a building was bound, whipped and burned at the stake. If the fire was accidental he or she had to repair the damage.

2   The vigiles were fire-fighters who patrolled the city – especially at night – to prevent fires breaking out and to arrest anyone who caused a fire.

3   The vigiles were also used to chase and capture runaway slaves.

4   Wealthy people travelled with a guard of slaves, especially at night, to protect them from robbery or attack.

5   City officials called aediles checked that householders kept the streets outside their homes clean and safe.

6   Aediles inspected shops to check that, for example, the bread being sold was the correct weight.

7   Landlords could be prosecuted if their buildings fell down.

8   Fighting between supporters of teams of chariot racers was common. The greatest rivals were the supporters of the Greens and the Blues.

9   Prisoners of war were used as slave labour to build new buildings such as the Colosseum.

10 Murderers were sentenced to death in the arena, fighting as gladiators until everyone had been killed.

11 Groups of youths, often from wealthy families, roamed the streets at night looking for a fight.

12 Windows were barred to prevent burglaries.

13 Anyone who was burgled had to try to stop the thief themselves, with the help of their friends, or collect evidence if they thought they knew who the thief was.

14 Minor crime was tried by a judge who could consult lawyers.

15 Major crime was tried by a jury.

3   Use the statements above to make three lists of:
   a   crimes
   b   punishments
   c   methods of preventing crime.

4   Using the information you have gathered, decide which of the following statements are true and which are false.
   a   Crime was kept firmly under control. It was not a problem.
   b   Roman laws were very detailed and covered many aspects of life.

   c   The Romans had an effective police force that investigated crimes and caught criminals.
   d   Roman laws were simple and not very detailed.
   e   The Romans had a simple system of punishments.
   f   The Romans had a complex system of punishments with fines, prison sentences and executions.
   g   There was no police force to investigate crime or arrest criminals.

5   From all you have found out, which story ending on page 14 do you now think is most likely? Do you want to change your view? Discuss your decision with the rest of the class.

The streets of Rome

This picture shows various aspects of Roman crime, punishments and policing. Try to match the descriptions on the previous page with the events in this picture.

To succeed in the exam you need to be able to support your answers with **contextual** knowledge. The activities so far should have helped you to see that:

- Roman laws were very detailed and covered many aspects of life
- there was no police force to investigate crime or arrest criminals
- Roman trials were fair. Minor crime was tried by a judge, major crime by a jury
- the Romans had a complex system of punishments with fines and executions.

But in an exam you should be able to give specific examples, precise names, facts and figures to back up a general statement. So you are going to practise. Use the information on these two pages to find information or evidence to back up these statements. Record them in your own copy of this table.

Statement	Supporting evidence
Roman laws were very detailed and covered many aspects of life	
There was no police force to investigate crime or arrest criminals	
Roman trials were fair. Minor crime was tried by a judge, major crime by a jury	
The Romans had a complex system of punishments with fines and executions	

Roman laws

Roman laws dealt with every possible crime, from assassinating the Emperor and murder to everyday crimes such as street theft and burglary. There were also laws to make Rome a better place in which to live. Laws said that householders had to keep the pavements and streets outside their homes clean. Dumping waste in the River Tiber (where drinking water came from) was illegal, and so was starting fires – there was always great danger of fire spreading rapidly and destroying hundreds of homes.

The first recorded Roman laws were the **Twelve Tables**, which were written down *c*.450BC. At school, children learned them by heart. Over the next 1,000 years many new laws were added as rulers tried to stop crimes. The greatest Roman law code was the work of the Emperor Justinian in AD533. Justinian brought all the different laws together, simplifying and organising them into one system. This was a great achievement but **Justinian's Digest** of the Roman laws was still one and a half times the length of the Bible!

Roman policing

In the early years of Rome there was no police force in the city. If a Roman was attacked or robbed then he had to rely on friends and neighbours to catch the attacker or thief. This often led to more violence. In AD6, Emperor Augustus set up three kinds of forces to police Rome. However, the situation did not change much.

The vigiles
There were 7,000 vigiles. They patrolled the streets and their duties combined fire-fighting, crime prevention and capturing runaway slaves.

Urban cohorts
There were 3,000 urban cohorts. They were soldiers. Their main job was to keep order by stopping riots. They did not patrol the streets.

Praetorian Guard
The Emperor's household guard were used only in emergencies to protect the Emperor from riots.

Do-it-yourself!
Stealing was regarded as a minor crime because it did not affect the ruler or the majority of the people. Even after the establishment of these different kinds of police forces if you were burgled you could not expect any of them to help you. You still had to find the criminal, collect the evidence and take the accused to court yourself.

Trials and courts

Minor crime

At the magistrates' court a judge was chosen – he was not a lawyer although he could take advice from lawyers – and both sides presented their evidence. Then the judge reached his decision.

Major crime

There was a slightly different system for more serious cases like murder. Cases were tried by magistrates but with a jury. Again, anyone could bring a case to court for trial. When the suspect appeared, both sides gave evidence and then the jury decided if he or she was guilty. The magistrate then decided the sentence.

Therefore there were three basic principles at work in Roman trials:

1 Any Roman citizen could bring a case to court.
2 The defendant was innocent until proved guilty.
3 The defendant had the right to present evidence.

Punishments

Imprisonment was not used as a punishment. Prisons were only for people in debt or who were awaiting trial or execution. Violent punishments were common. Anyone convicted of patricide (killing his father) was tied in a sack with a number of snakes and thrown into the river to drown. Over time, Roman punishments became more violent, including amputating limbs, death by pouring molten lead down the convicted person's throat, and crucifixion for those, like Christians and Jews, who refused to recognise the Emperor as a god.

Punishments for citizens (ordinary Romans)

Citizens could be put to death for serious crimes such as:

arson

attacking the Emperor

robbing temples

stealing farm animals

Punishment for lesser crimes such as theft or selling under-weight bread included:

whipping

repaying the cost of goods

confiscation of property

Punishments for nobles

Nobles could be sentenced to death for serious crimes but they were allowed to go into exile and avoid prosecution.

Punishments for slaves

All the slaves in a household were crucified if one of them murdered or tried to murder their master.

Slaves could give evidence at a trial, but only if they had been tortured first!

Punishments for legionnaires

Legionnaires who ran away in battle faced execution. In addition, one in every ten men from the legion that they ran away from was chosen by lot and also executed. This decimation was carried out ruthlessly.

Smarter Revision: Memory maps

You're only just starting the course but we're already thinking about helping you to revise. Revision isn't something you tack on to the end of a course. It's something you should build up as you go along – and that makes it much easier. For your main activity on the Roman period, you are going to build a memory map, and then it'll be ready to help you revise later in the course. How about that for saving time?

How can a map save you time and boost your memory?

- Memory maps encourage you to link pieces of information together. You learn more by making links, because it makes you think!
- You are actively involved with your revision. This is much better than simply reading, hoping your brain will act as a sponge and soak up the information!

Your own images, colours and acronyms will help your memory.

- Memory maps are a flexible tool for revision. You can produce a memory map from memory, check it against the original, then add in what you have missed.
- Finally, and perhaps most importantly, memory maps make revision a lot more interesting!

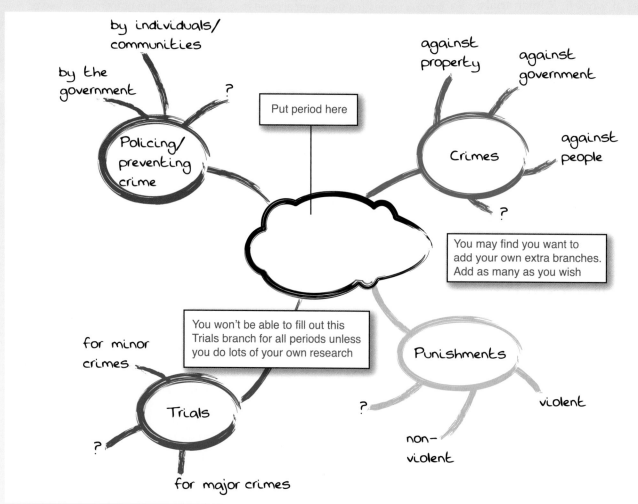

How to build your Roman memory map

Step 1: Use plain A4 or, even better, A3 paper (landscape). Space is important. The end result should not look too busy or cramped.

Step 2: Copy the map on page 20 to get you started.

Step 3: As you work through this section add more information to the map. Use pencil so that you can make any corrections that are needed. Remember:

- Use key words or phrases. Do not write full sentences.
- Use pictures/images/diagrams to replace or emphasise words. Lots of you will find it easier to remember visual images than words.
- PRINT words to make them stand out.

Step 4: When you have finished:

- Redraft your map to make sure everything is clear.
- Draw your own central picture which sums up the topic for you.

Using acronyms to help you remember

Roman **C**itizens **P**ay **T**o **P**ee. This is an acronym to help you remember the letters R, C, P, T and P. Why do you need to remember them?

Acronyms are a good example of fun revision – revision doesn't have to be boring. In fact it's difficult to learn anything if you're bored because you don't concentrate well. Inventing your own acronyms can help you to remember key pieces of information. The odder the acronym the more likely you are to remember it.

smarter revision tip

Memory maps are a really good way of revising big topics. Use them to help you revise the other sections of this book.

Meet the Examiner: Introducing Development Study questions

By now you should feel like an expert on Roman crime and punishment! However, simply knowing a lot is not enough to achieve a good grade in your GCSE. This page begins our advice on how to do really well.

You will sit two exams for your OCR GCSE in History.

Paper 1 is a two hour exam which is divided into two parts:

*   Section A covers the **Development Study** your school has chosen to study – in this case Crime and Punishment Through Time.

*   Section B covers the **Study in Depth** your school has chosen to study.

Paper 2 is a **Historical Source Investigation.** We will explore this exam later in the book. (See pages 74–75 and 118–119.)

The exam paper below gives you an idea of what Section A of Paper 1 will look like.

Section A: Development Study
Crime and Punishment Through Time

You are advised to spend about 1 hour on this section.

Answer Question 1 and ONE other question.

1   Study the sources carefully and then answer the questions that follow.

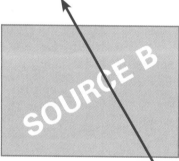

(a) Study Source A. Are you surprised that these crimes could be punished by the death penalty? Use the source and your knowledge to explain your answer.   [5]

(b) Study Source B. How far does this source give an accurate impression of eighteenth-century smugglers? Use the source and your knowledge to explain your answer.   [5]

(c) Study Source C. Does this source prove that transportation was a failure? Use the source and your knowledge to explain your answer.   [5]

A   TIMING

It is important that you try to stick to one hour for this section. If you spend too much time on Section A it will leave you short of time for Section B (the Study in Depth), which is worth slightly more marks – so time yourself carefully.

B   ANSWERING QUESTION 1

You must answer this question. It is based on a group of sources. It has three parts, worth a total of 15 marks. Aim to spend about 25 minutes of your hour on this question.

22

C THINK CAREFULLY ABOUT WHICH QUESTION YOU CHOOSE

After you have answered question 1 you need to make an important choice. You will have three questions to choose from (we have given just one here, as an example). Each question is worth 20 marks and is broken down into three parts. You should aim to spend about 35–40 minutes on this question.

Do not rush your decision. Read **all three** parts of each question before you make your choice. It is important that you can answer all three parts of the question, not just the first part which only carries 5 marks.

D LOOK AT THE THEME OF THE QUESTION

Each question will have a theme that links the three parts of the question together. Question 2 is exploring how far attitudes to crime and punishment have changed over time.

You must answer ALL parts of the question you choose.

2 Some attitudes about crime and punishment have changed over the years.

(a) Briefly describe ways in which the Romans punished criminals.   [5]

(b) Explain why the story of Robin Hood was popular in the Middle Ages.   [7]

(c) 'The treatment of criminals in the nineteenth century was different from their treatment in the Middle Ages.' Explain how far you agree with this statement.   [8]

E 'DESCRIBE' QUESTIONS

The first part of the question is worth 5 marks. It asks you to *briefly describe* something from a period. This might be the work of an individual, a particular type of crime, or a form of punishment.

F 'EXPLAIN' QUESTIONS

The second part of the question is worth 7 marks. You will be asked to explain how or why something has happened. You need to spend longer answering 'Explain' questions than 'Describe' questions. Question 2b is asking you to explain people's attitudes to the story of Robin Hood.

G 'EVALUATION' QUESTIONS

The third part of the question is worth 8 marks. You will usually be asked to evaluate a statement and explain how far you agree or disagree with it. This question could require you to bring in knowledge from a long period of time or to set a development in its period context.

The examiners are not trying to catch you out in the exam: they are giving you a chance to show what you know – **and what you can do with what you know**. If you work out what the question is getting at, you will be able to answer it from what you have learned.

 To make sure you stay relevant to the questions you will need to practise how to 'decode' them.

Decoding exam questions

Step 1: Read the question a couple of times.

Step 2: Highlight each of the following. You could use a different colour for each.

> **Date boundaries** – What time period should you cover in your answer? Stick to this carefully, otherwise you will waste time writing about events that are not relevant to the question.
>
> **Content focus** – The topic the examiner wants you to focus on.
>
> **Question type** – Different question types require different approaches. Look for key words like 'Describe' or 'Explain'; these will help you work out what type of approach is needed.
>
> **Marks available** – Look at how many marks the question is worth. This gives you a guide as to how much you are expected to write. Do not spend too long on questions that are only worth a few marks.

Look at the exam question below.

You must stick to the date boundaries of the question. In this case it is the Roman period. Details of how crime and punishment in other time periods progressed will not gain you extra marks.

The content focus for this question is on how the Romans tried to prevent crime. This must be the focus of your answer. There is no need to explore other areas of Roman justice such as trials. Stick to policing and punishments.

Briefly describe how the Romans tried to prevent crime.

[5 marks]

You need to 'describe how' the Romans tried to prevent crime. You are not being asked to 'explain why' they introduced measures to try and prevent crime or whether you think they were successful.

5 marks are available. This indicates that only a short answer is required. One paragraph would be enough.

Tackling 'describe' questions

Tip 1: Avoid general statements. Make sure you show off your knowledge and give specific examples.

Describe questions carry only 5 marks. It is important that you get to the point quickly and avoid 'waffly' general statements that do not pick up many marks. Look at the example below:

> The Romans believed that it was very important to try and prevent some crimes. They introduced lots of different things to try and stop crime and they had harsh punishments.

This answer contains **general statements**. It provides no specific details of how the Romans tried to prevent crime. It would score only 1 mark.

This answer below is a lot better. It gives specific examples of what the Romans did to prevent crime.

> The Romans did try to prevent some crimes. They were particularly worried about fires. They had a police force, men called vigiles, whose main duty was patrolling and putting out fires. Also the Romans used harsh public punishments to deter others. Roman citizens could be put to death in public if found guilty of arson. This was meant to scare others and stop them starting fires in the future.

Tip 2: Stay relevant to the question.

One of the main problems with 'Describe' questions is that pupils often write too much! They include details that are not relevant to the question. You do *not* need to explain why they introduced measures or evaluate how successful they were. Questions that ask you to explain and evaluate are worth more marks – we will tackle these later on.

Activity

Read the answer below. The student has written too much because he has not stayed relevant to the question. He has:

- tried to explain why the Romans tried to introduce policing methods
- explored the area of trials when the question refers to crime prevention
- added in other irrelevant knowledge.
  On your own copy, cross out the sentences that are irrelevant to the question. You should be left with a good answer!

> Roman rulers needed loyal and obedient citizens to keep the Empire strong. They thought long and hard about how to prevent crime in Rome and the rest of the Empire. The Romans had a very large Empire, partly because they had an effective army. They were worried about some aspects of crime. They invested quite a lot of effort in trying to prevent fires and riots. It is arguable how effective they were in achieving these aims. They had a form of policemen, called vigiles, whose main duty was patrolling the streets, looking for potential fire risks. They put out the fires that they found. Vigiles also chased runaway slaves – this was important to many rich Romans who viewed slaves as property.
>
> The Roman rulers were more worried about riots than stopping crime. Over a million people lived in the thriving city of Rome. Really rich people lived in beautiful villas whilst the poor lived in cramped small flats. The rulers were worried about losing control. They sent urban cohorts to stop riots, but these well-trained soldiers did not patrol the streets.
>
> There was a sensible system of trials in ancient Rome. Magistrates acted as judges and tried minor crimes. The magistrate listened to both sides then made his decision. There was a slightly different system for more serious cases like murder. Cases were tried by magistrates but this time with a jury. Anyone could bring a case to court for trial. When the suspect appeared, both sides gave evidence and then the jury decided if he or she was guilty. The magistrate then decided the sentence.
>
> Also the Romans used harsh public punishments to deter others. Roman citizens could be put to death in public if found guilty of arson. This was meant to scare others and stop them starting fires in the future. They also attempted to deter people from minor crimes. People found guilty of selling underweight bread or stealing were publicly whipped.

Section 3: Crime and punishment in the Middle Ages

In about AD500 the Roman Empire in Western Europe collapsed, destroyed by tribes from Germany and the east. Roman systems of dealing with crime and punishment fell out of use. Britain was settled by several Saxon tribes, each with their own laws and customs, quite different from those of the Romans.

We now enter a new time period historians call the Middle Ages, which is often sub-divided into Saxon England, Norman England and the later Middle Ages. People often think that crimes and punishments in the Middle Ages were bloodthirsty, and that justice was simple and didn't change at all. Your two main tasks in this section are to find out:
a) if justice in the Middle Ages was bloody and thoughtless, and b) to see how much justice changed between 500 and 1500.

Activities

1 Work in pairs. You have five minutes. What evidence can you find in the picture below of:
   a different crimes
   b different punishments
   c different forms of policing and/or crime prevention
   d different trials.
2 You now have three minutes. How many similarities can you find between crime, punishment, trials and policing in the Middle Ages and crime, punishment, trials and policing in the Roman period?
3 Now you have two minutes. What differences can you find between crime, punishment, trials and policing in the Middle Ages and in the Roman period?
4 List any questions that you have about justice in the Middle Ages.

Criminal moment in time 2: Saxon village c.AD650

26

27

3.1 How much changed between 500 and 1500?

These two pages summarise the main developments in crime and punishment that you will be studying in more detail. You will learn about the main features of crime and punishment in the Saxon period, the Norman period and at the end of the Middle Ages.

	Impact of the fall of the Roman Empire 410–450	The Saxons 450–1066
Crime	The Roman legions left in 410. Anglo-Saxon tribes from what is now Germany saw Britain as wealthy – and undefended. Groups of raiders, invaders and settlers came looking for what they could seize. For a while, crimes such as theft and murder increased, until Anglo-Saxon law and order took over – see column 2.	Most crime was theft of money, food and belongings, usually low in value. Violent crimes were a small minority of cases.
Policing	After 410 Roman law and order did not collapse at once. The Roman civilians who were left behind tried to keep Roman methods of policing going. But without the soldiers to back them up, Roman systems gradually failed to operate.	The victims of crime were expected to find the criminals themselves, calling fellow villagers to chase the criminals (**hue and cry**). Adult men were grouped into tens called **tithings**. If one of them broke the law the others had to bring him to court.
Punishment	Punishment needs the threat of force behind it. Without the support of the legions, the Romans left behind could not enforce Roman laws and after a while the very different Anglo-Saxon systems of punishment took their place.	Criminals paid compensation to their victims. This was called **wergild** – the blood price. Only a few offences carried the death penalty. Prisons were only used to hold the accused awaiting trial.
Trials	Roman trials only worked when everyone understood how they worked and there were the legions to enforce their decisions. Anglo-Saxons had no knowledge of how Roman trials took place and soon enforced their own way of making legal decisions.	Juries of local people decided whether the accused was innocent or guilty. If they couldn't decide then the accused underwent **trial by ordeal** where God decided whether he or she was innocent.

Activity

How much changed?

Compare the descriptions of crime, policing, punishment and trials in the Saxon period, the Norman period and the later Middle Ages. If total change is 10 and no change is 0, think about each topic (crime, policing, punishment and trials) and write down how you would rank it out of 10 and explain your score. As you work through this chapter you will find out more about each topic and you can decide if you still agree with your score.

The Normans 1066–c.1200	Later Middle Ages c.1200–1500
Most crime was theft of money, food and belongings, usually low in value. Violent crimes were a small minority of cases.	Most crime was theft of money, food and belongings, usually low in value. Violent crimes were a small minority of cases.
The victims of crime were expected to find the criminals themselves, calling fellow villagers to chase the criminals (hue and cry). Adult men were grouped into tens called tithings. If one of them broke the law the others had to bring him to court.	The hue and cry and tithings were still used. Other government officials such as the county coroner and the sheriff played a leading role in investigating some crimes. Leading villagers were appointed as constables to help keep order.
Norman kings believed that any crime was an insult to the king's peace. They ended the system of wergild, and punishments emphasised the power of the king rather than compensating the victim. Fines were now paid to the king and serious criminals were executed or mutilated. Prisons were still only used to hold the accused awaiting trial.	Execution and other physical punishments were still the most common form of punishment. Fines were still paid to the king. Prisons were still only used to hold the accused awaiting trial.
Juries of local people decided whether the accused was innocent or guilty. If they couldn't decide then the accused still underwent trial by ordeal where God decided whether he or she was innocent. By 1100 a series of courts had developed. Royal courts and shire courts met twice a year to deal with serious cases. Village or manor courts were held weekly by every landowner.	Juries still decided cases. Trial by ordeal was abolished in 1215. The system of courts developed further. Royal judges travelled around the country dealing with serious cases. County courts were held by Justices of the Peace who were leading local landowners. Each manor still had its own court held by the local lord, often once a week.

3.2 Was justice in the Middle Ages bloody and thoughtless?

Some people think of the Middle Ages as a bloody, cruel and superstitious time. But were the Middle Ages really like that? In this enquiry you will be examining medieval punishment, policing and trials. You have two questions to consider:

* Were punishments in the Middle Ages bloody?
* Were policing and trials arbitrary and thoughtless?

As you study the different types of **punishment**, you will think about where they fit on this line:

Bloody   Mild

As you study the different systems of **policing** and **trials**, you will also need to keep asking yourself about how much thought went into policing and trials. The line below will help you. Think about where the different types of policing and trial will fit.

Thoughtless   Thoughtful

Activity

To get started, read Cedric's story on page 31 and decide how you think Cedric will be punished. This is a story based on evidence from the Laws of King Ethelbert of Kent in 603. It describes a very common crime – physical assault. Your task is to try and predict what punishment you think Cedric will face.

Option 1
Cedric will have his left hand chopped off. This will act as a reminder to him that he shouldn't use physical violence. It will also deter others who might think that attacking one's neighbour is acceptable.

Option 2
Cedric will be ordered to pay Harold 12 shillings for a broken thigh. Cedric is lucky he didn't break Harold's thumb. The fine for that is 20 shillings.

Option 3
Cedric will be executed even though this is his first offence. He acted in anger and caused a fellow villager to suffer potential starvation. After all, Harold will not be able to farm his field. His family may suffer starvation next year. This is the ultimate deterrent.

As you work through this enquiry you will find out what punishment Cedric actually faced. You are also going to prepare for, and play, a game that will help you understand the different elements of Saxon justice. It will also help to improve your revision skills and examination technique. And it might even be fun too!

How will Cedric be punished?

Cedric was worried. He couldn't remember the last time the sun had shone. Rain, rain, rain. This was meant to be the spring. When was he going to sow his corn? If the rain continued there would be no harvest this year. He was sure of it. How was he going to feed his family? Would they starve?

Cedric knew one thing: his neighbour Harold wouldn't help out. Cedric felt that it was always he who supported Harold in times of need. He was always lending Harold his tools. After all, it was the neighbourly thing to do. Times were hard and it was important for everyone in the village to pull together. But Harold rarely returned Cedric's tools. In any case, when he did they were often broken. Some people are just no good, Cedric thought to himself. It was just then that his son came rushing in, looking outraged.

'Harold has taken our ox and is using it to plough his field,' said his son, catching his breath. This was the last straw.

'He needs to be taught a lesson', Cedric thought to himself. He grabbed his axe and marched down the muddy track. The rain blurred his vision. In front of him, he could just make out Harold – guiding Cedric's prize ox and ploughing expertly.

Rage took over. Cedric saw red. He charged at Harold with his axe, swinging it straight into Harold's thigh. Then, just to ensure Harold understood him,

Cedric stamped his foot on Harold's leg before pulling the axe out. Harold's screams could be heard from the other side of the village. People ran to the scene to find out what had happened.

Cedric's rage only left him when he got back to his house. He leaned his axe, now smeared in his neighbour's blood, against the wall. He was worried. He knew that it was only a matter of time before he would have to appear in court. He couldn't bear to think about his punishment … if only he could control his temper!

For your GCSE you need to develop your recall skills. You need to be able to remember *a lot of information*. You also need to bring the relevant information to the front of your mind. Smarter Revision gives you tips to help.

Tip 1: Making cards

Revision cards are clear and to the point. As you work through the next 24 pages you are going to make a set of cards that you can use to play a game – and use to revise! On these two pages we guide you through the process of making the cards as you find out about Saxon punishments.

Blood feud

When the Romans left England, tribes from Germany came to settle here. Some were known as Angles, others as Saxons. They set up small tribal kingdoms. The Anglo-Saxons were farmers who believed in being loyal – loyal to your family and loyal to your lord. This led to a basic system of justice, based on revenge. Early Saxon kings allowed the victims of crime to punish criminals themselves. If someone was murdered, the family had the right to track down and kill the murderer. This right was known as blood feud.

Early Saxon kings used blood feud because they came from a warrior class where violence was acceptable and they didn't consider it their job to settle arguments between families. Also, kings couldn't pay for a police force because they didn't raise regular taxes. Blood feud was meant to be so fierce that it would deter people from committing crimes.

But blood feud only led to more bloodshed. It often meant that families banded together to take revenge for an attack. This then led to another attack, and a cycle of violence began. Blood feud wasn't workable in the long run. It relied on people wanting to use violence, and some wanted a peaceful solution instead.

Activities

Card 1

1 You need to make the first card for your game. To do well in the exam, you need to be able to **describe** what Saxon justice was like. You also need to be able to **explain** why they chose this particular type of justice. Making cards will help you to understand the difference between describing and explaining.

BLOOD FEUD

Description — Describe how it worked and how it was meant to keep the peace.

Explanation — Explain why they used it. What problems did it cause?

Changes — When you make your cards remember to leave room at the bottom of each card like this as you will be adding to it later to show how this aspect of crime and punishment changed.

2 Your other task is deciding if punishments were bloody. Where would you put the card on this line?

Bloody ←——————→ Mild

Saxon policing

There was no police force in Saxon England. Kings did not regularly collect taxes, so they couldn't pay for a professional police force. By the tenth century, they had set up a different kind of self-help system known as a **tithing**. The Anglo-Saxons were warriors and farmers who valued loyalty. Tithings were based on loyalty – loyalty to your family, and loyalty to your friends. A tithing was a group of ten people. All males over the age of twelve had to belong to a tithing. Anyone accused of a crime had to pay a sum of money to the head of the tithing. If one member of the tithing broke the law, the others had to bring him to court, or pay a fine.

The idea behind tithings was to stop crime by making people responsible for one another. This was a form of **collective responsibility**. It was much more effective than blood feud because people didn't want to let their family and friends down – and they didn't want to pay a fine for someone else's crime. This meant they would make sure the men in their tithing obeyed the law. This helped to reduce crime.

The Saxons had another system of policing called the 'hue and cry'. This was simply a larger version of tithings. If the victim of a crime raised the hue and cry by calling out for help, the entire village had to down tools and join in the hunt to find the criminal. If they didn't, the whole village had to pay a hefty fine given by the local court.

The Saxons were used to protecting each other in this way. The hue and cry was also based on loyalty –

loyalty to the village. It bound everyone together. Saxon kings understood the importance of keeping the peace; they knew people didn't want to pay a fine. The hue and cry seems quite sensible. It wasn't just the victim of the crime who had to find the lawbreaker. The whole village had to get involved. This made the chances of being caught much greater.

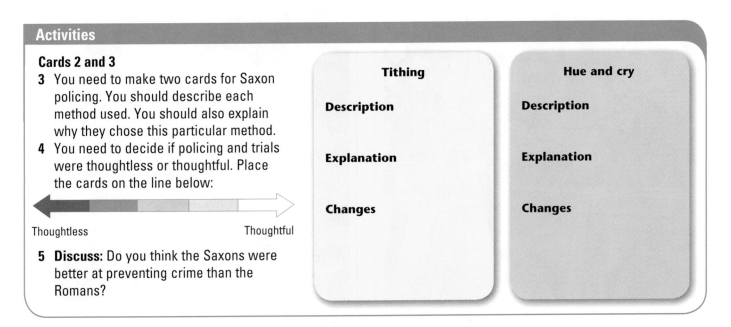

Activities

Cards 2 and 3

3 You need to make two cards for Saxon policing. You should describe each method used. You should also explain why they chose this particular method.

4 You need to decide if policing and trials were thoughtless or thoughtful. Place the cards on the line below:

Thoughtless ← → Thoughtful

5 **Discuss:** Do you think the Saxons were better at preventing crime than the Romans?

Tithing	Hue and cry
Description	Description
Explanation	Explanation
Changes	Changes

Saxon trial by jury

If someone was accused of a crime, the local village would decide if the accused was guilty or innocent. This was because people lived in small close-knit communities. They were loyal to one another and worked together to make sure that people obeyed the law. They used a form of trial by jury. The jury was made up of men from the village who knew both the accuser and the accused. The victim would summon the accused to appear in court. If he didn't appear, he lost the case and paid the compensation. If he failed to pay, he was declared an outlaw. This meant that he no longer had the protection of the king's laws. Anyone could legally attack him or kill him.

Both the accuser and the accused told their version of events to the jury. It was then up to the jury to decide who was telling the truth. If no eyewitness saw the crime take place, the jury had to use their experience of the people concerned to decide on innocence or guilt. If the jury felt that the accuser was being more honest than the accused, they swore an oath that the accused was guilty. This oath taking was called **compurgation**.

Oath taking was a very serious business. The Saxons believed that swearing a false oath was the same as lying to God. Therefore a priest was always involved in this oath taking.

Trial by hot iron

This was usually taken by women. The accused had to carry a piece of red-hot iron for three metres. Her hand was then bandaged and unwrapped three days later. If the wound was not healing everyone would know that God was saying she was guilty. But if the wound was healing cleanly, God had found her innocent.

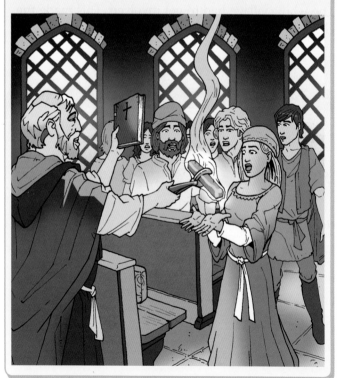

Trial by cold water

This was usually taken by men. The accused was lowered into the water (either a river or a pond as close to the church as possible) on the end of a rope. The rope was knotted above the waist. If the person sank and the knot went below the surface of the water, the person was innocent because the 'pure water' had been willing to let this innocent person beneath its surface. However, if he and the knot floated he was guilty because the water was rejecting him.

The pictures on this spread show some of the different types of trial by ordeal. There were times when the jury could not decide if the accused was guilty or innocent. If this was the case the solution was to let God decide. Humans might not know the truth but an all-seeing God would. Therefore the accused faced a trial by ordeal. There were four different types of ordeal. All trials except trial by cold water took place inside a church. Before each trial a careful religious ritual was followed. The accused would have to fast for three days, then hear mass in church. As each trial began the priest would read a religious passage.

Trial by hot water

This was also taken by men. The accused put his hand into boiling water to pick up an object, sometimes a ring, and lifted it out. The arm was then bandaged. Three days later the bandage was taken off. If the wound was healing cleanly the person was innocent.

Trial by 'blessed' bread

This was taken by priests. The priest first had to pray, asking that he be choked by the bread if he lied. Then he had to eat a piece of consecrated (blessed) bread. If he choked on the bread he was guilty.

Activities

1 In groups, discuss the following questions:
   a How do trial by jury and trial by ordeal show that the Saxons were religious?
   b Does trial by ordeal show that the Saxons were thoughtful when it came to trying people?

2 Make two revision cards for Saxon trials. You need to be able to describe what each trial was like. You also need to be able to explain why the Saxons used this particular method.

3 Place each trial on the line below:

Thoughtless   Thoughtful

Name of the trial

Description

Explanation

Changes

Saxon punishments

By about AD700, England was divided into a smaller number of kingdoms ruled by fewer but more powerful kings. They understood the importance of making sure their laws were obeyed. These kings realised the main part of their job was to protect their people. This led to a more peaceful country. They stopped the violence of blood feud and introduced a more peaceful alternative, the wergild. This was a system of fines, paid to the victims of crime in the form of compensation. Wergild was paid if someone was murdered, or if someone was injured in a physical assault.

With the introduction of wergild, the chance of further violence was much less likely and the number of violent attacks decreased. Saxon laws became very detailed about the fines criminals had to pay. But it was an unequal system. The wergild for killing a noble was 300 shillings; the wergild for killing a freeman was 100 shillings, while the fine for killing a free peasant was even lower.

Activities

Discuss:

1 Some of the wounds in Source 1 have not been given a price. Can you work out the missing wergilds?

2 Does this help you to work out how Cedric (from page 31) would be punished?

3 What do you think was the purpose of punishing re-offenders (see page 37) so harshly?

Source 1

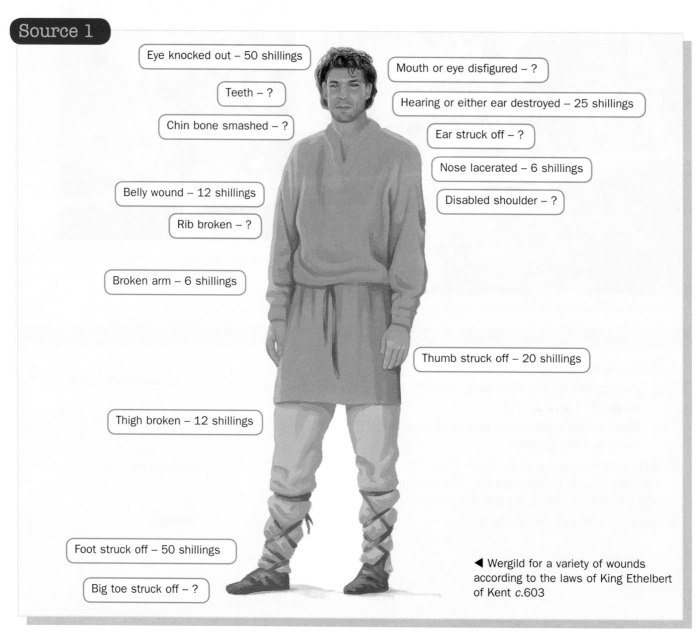

Eye knocked out – 50 shillings

Teeth – ?

Chin bone smashed – ?

Mouth or eye disfigured – ?

Hearing or either ear destroyed – 25 shillings

Ear struck off – ?

Nose lacerated – 6 shillings

Belly wound – 12 shillings

Disabled shoulder – ?

Rib broken – ?

Broken arm – 6 shillings

Thumb struck off – 20 shillings

Thigh broken – 12 shillings

Foot struck off – 50 shillings

Big toe struck off – ?

◀ Wergild for a variety of wounds according to the laws of King Ethelbert of Kent c.603

Not all crimes were punishable by fines. Some crimes were seen as so serious that they carried the death penalty, for example, treason against the king and betraying your lord. As you know, Saxon society was based on loyalty. Acting against the king or betraying your lord was breaking this tie of loyalty. For the law to work well, and for kings to protect their people, they knew that everyone had to be loyal to one another. The death penalty was meant to show people the importance of loyalty.

Re-offenders were also punished harshly if they were caught. Punishment for regular offenders included mutilation, for example cutting off a hand, ear or nose or 'putting out' the eyes.

Prisons were rarely used in Saxon England because they were expensive. Prisons would have to be built, gaolers would have to be paid, and prisoners fed. This was impossible at a time when kings only collected taxes for wars. Prisons were only used for holding the accused before trial. This ensured that serious criminals didn't escape. It meant they were much more likely to face justice.

Source 2

▲ The prison (the small building on the bridge) at Bradford-on-Avon in Wiltshire is one of the earliest surviving in Britain.

smarter revision tips

You could use a **memory map** to pull together all you know about Saxon justice. See pages 20–21 to remind you how to draw your own memory map. The main branches could be: Crime, Policing, Punishment and Trials.

Can you think of any good **acronyms** to help you remember some of the detail?

Activities

4 Make four revision cards for Saxon punishments. You need to be able to describe each method. You also need to be able to explain why they chose this particular method.

Name of the punishment

Description

Explanation

Changes

5 Place the methods of punishments on the line below:

Thoughtless ←——————————→ Thoughtful

Tip 1: Making cards

Making the cards for your game has been a good way to make revision notes. The cards are clear and to the point.

Tip 2: Using pictures

Using pictures can also help trigger your memory. Have you ever heard the saying, 'a picture paints a thousand words'? Let's put this to the test. What form of Saxon crime prevention do you think the card on the right shows?

Draw pictures on the back of your cards. Your simple picture should describe the aspect on the card. This will help trigger your memory.

Tip 3: Testing yourself

Another good way to revise is to test yourself. Take each card. Read what it says, then turn it over. In your own words:

- describe what the crime prevention policy was
- explain why they used it.
- Now check to see if you were correct.

Repeat this for all of your cards. The pictures on the back should help jog your memory.

The What? and Why? game

It is now time to play the **What? and Why?** game. The aim of the game is to try to win six points for each card. The winner is the person who gets the most points at the end. Have your cards facing down. Take it in turns to lift a card – show your partner the image on the back of the card. Ask them to talk about the card. They score:

- two points if they can describe the method (what?)
- four points if they can also explain why it was used and how it worked (why?)
- you can award six points if they can also explain whether it was bloody or mild, or thoughtless or thoughtful.

Now that you've worked out how to make smarter revision cards, and play the What? and Why? game, you can use them both at any point during the rest of the course.

Both exam papers contain questions that test your ability to use visual and written sources effectively. Have a look at this sample exam question:

1 Study Source A. What can you learn from this source about trial by ordeal in the Middle Ages. Use the source and your knowledge to explain your answer.

Source A: A medieval illustration of trial by ordeal

To get high marks you must do more than just describe what you can see in the source – you must also explain it and look beyond it.

Step 1

Identify the clues in the source that can help you answer the question. You could highlight the fact that trial by ordeal was a religious trial as there is someone on the left holding a bible. Also that the ordeal in this case was being submerged in water.

Step 2

Use your knowledge of the topic to go beyond the obvious clues and **explain what the source is saying** about the role of God in this trial. Ask yourself: What do I know that can help me make sense of this evidence? What can I **infer** from this source?

This type of question is often known as an inference question. They are usually worth either 5 or 6 marks so you should not spend too long on these questions. The key thing to remember is to stick to the focus of the task and use your knowledge of this to make inferences.

- Only bring in your own knowledge if it is relevant to the question and helps to explain the meaning of a source. The focus here is on trial by ordeal in the Middle Ages so there is no need to impress the examiner with your knowledge of policing systems in the Saxon period! You will not gain any extra marks as it is not what the question asks.
- Stick to what you can learn from the source. There is no need to evaluate how trustworthy the source is. If you do, you will waste valuable time and pick up no extra marks.

Activity

1 Read the student answer below. Note how the student identifies key details and then explains what they say about trial by ordeal. Now complete the answer.

In source A there are at least five people watching a trial by ordeal. <u>This suggests</u> that the trial by ordeal was important because local people were present. The five people may well have been members of the jury. We know that trial by ordeal was only used when a jury couldn't decide. They might not be able to decide on guilt but God could. The source shows the accused being lowered into water with their hands and feet tied. <u>This could suggest</u> that trial by ordeal was harsh and unfair. If the accused floated they were guilty and if they didn't they were innocent. This seems unfair to us but it was logical to the people of the Middle Ages because God was deciding. There is a priest on the left who is reading from a book – the Bible. <u>This suggests</u> ...

3.3 Did William totally change Saxon justice?

In Source 1 the historian Simon Schama is describing the Battle of Hastings where the Norman Duke William defeated King Harold Godwinson. William went on to be crowned King and take control of England. Simon Schama suggests that William totally changed Saxon laws and justice. Use these information panels to decide if you agree with him.

Source 1

In 2001, Professor Simon Schama, in his TV series *A History of Britain*, stood on Senlac Hill and proclaimed:

There are times and places where history comes at you with a rush, violent, decisive and bloody; a truck load of trouble. **Wiping out** everything that gives you your bearings in the world: **law, customs, loyalty** and **language**. And Hastings is one of those places … **Here, one king of England was annihilated and another king of England set up in his place**.

1 William destroyed people's homes to make way for new castles. Many Saxons suffered. Some Saxons became angry with their Norman conquerors and fought back, sometimes killing Norman soldiers. William ordered that if any Norman was murdered all the people of the region had to join together to pay a hefty fine. It was called the Murdrum fine.

2 William decided the laws of the Saxon kings should be retained. He therefore kept Saxon trial by jury, tithings and the hue and cry.

3 The Normans introduced another form of trial by ordeal – trial by combat. The accused fought the accuser until one was beaten or killed. The loser was then hanged as he had been found guilty by God.

4 The Normans retained the religious ritual of Saxon trial by ordeal.

5 William used the death penalty for serious crimes.

6 William used fines for lesser crimes. He ordered that fines should be paid to the king's officials and not to the victims as compensation.

William introduced new laws. He introduced the hated Forest Laws. Trees could not be cut down for fuel or for building. People in the forests were forbidden to own dogs or bows and arrows. The punishment for hunting deer was to be blinded.

7

The Anglo-Saxons gave women almost equal rights in law with men. Norman law, based on Roman law, was much harsher on women.

Source 2

8

11th century legal text

Women's authority is nil. Let her in all things be subject to the rule of men. She cannot be a witness in court, nor sit in judgement.

Activities

To do well in the exam you need to be able to write good explanations. This activity will help you with this.

1 Read the panels 1–8. Match them up to the following explanations **a–e**.

   a This was a change. William introduced this because he was religious and believed that God should decide who was guilty. The Normans were also a warrior nation and trial by battle had been an old Norman custom.

   b This was a change because the Murdrum fine was a new punishment. It was paid to the king instead of the victim. It was introduced to try to deter the Saxons from harming their new Norman lords. However, this could also be seen as continuity. It was simply a larger version of a tithing, or the hue and cry. It was meant to deter everyone in the region from attacking the Normans.

   c This law was changed because William and his Norman friends loved to hunt. If the Saxons killed deer, there wouldn't be enough for the Normans to hunt. If trees were cut down, there would be fewer wooded areas for the deer.

   d This was continuity. William believed the old king, Edward the Confessor, had promised him the throne. By keeping Edward's laws he was showing respect to the old king, and that he was Edward's rightful heir. In any case, he realised that 5,000 Norman knights couldn't keep control of 1.5 million Saxons. The Saxons already had an effective system of policing in place.

   e William changed fines because he believed that crimes were committed against the king's peace, rather than against the individual. This was also a useful way to increase his income.

2 Three of the panels do not have explanations. You need to write your own.

3 Draw your own table like the one below and decide where each panel and its explanation belongs.

4 How much change did William make? If 10 is 'huge changes' and 0 is 'no changes', give William a rating out of 10.

5 Why do you think that William did not completely change laws or punishments?

6 Look back at Simon Schama's opinion (Source 1). How far do you agree with him that English laws and customs were 'wiped out' after the Battle of Hastings?

	Change	Continuity	Change and continuity
Laws			
Punishments			
Trials			
Policing			
Amount of crime			

 Look at the question below. Remember what you learned about decoding exam questions on page 24.

You must stick to the date boundaries of the question. In this case it is just after 1066. Details of the changes made in the later Middle Ages are not relevant.

The content focus for this question is on **changes** made by William the Conqueror. **Do not** explore the aspects of **continuity**.

Explain why, after 1066, William the Conqueror changed some aspects of the system of law and order.

[7 marks]

You need to **explain** why William changed some **aspects** of law and order. A list of changes is not enough. Use the advice below to help you write effective explanations.

7 marks are available. You need to write more than you would for a 'Describe' question worth 5 marks. You will need to explain more than one change made by William. Aim for three paragraphs. Each paragraph should explain why William changed the system of law and order.

Writing effective explanations

Step 1: Identify the range of changes that William introduced

Use the cards that you have produced on the Saxons and Norman conquest to help you. Alternatively, you could use the continuity/change table on page 41.

Step 2: Select two or three areas to write about

Do not try and cover everything! Choose two or three areas where you are confident that you can **explain** the reasons why William changed things.

Step 3: Use connectives to tie in what you know to the question

Do not only describe the change, give reasons for it too. You can do this by using connectives such as 'this meant that … ', 'this led to … ' and 'this resulted in … ' to explain the reason behind the change.

Activity

Look at the answer below. The student has used connectives to explain why William changed one aspect of law and order. That's one paragraph done. Now have a go yourself at producing another paragraph that explains why William chose to change some aspects of Saxon law and order.

After the Norman invasion, William the Conqueror decided to change a few aspects of law and order. For example William used fines for lesser crimes. He ordered that fines should be paid to the king's officials instead of to the victims as compensation. William changed fines because he believed that crimes were committed against the king's peace, rather than against the individual. This meant that his authority was strengthened as people realised how important William was. This also led to an increase in his income.

3.4 Did religion make justice in the Middle Ages less bloody and thoughtless?

We have already seen that religion played an important part in medieval law, through trial by ordeal, which depended on trusting to God to make the decision (see pages 34–35). But there was more to the Church's role in justice than that. Your task is to weigh up: Was the Church's influence on justice a good thing?

Benefit of clergy

Anyone who was a member of the Church had the right – the benefit – to be tried in a special church court, presided over by the local bishop. Punishments in church courts often seemed to be lighter: being sent on a pilgrimage, or being made to confess your crime in front of everyone in the local church on Sunday.

Church courts had been intended to protect priests in the days when ordinary courts were rough and ready. But benefit of clergy was sometimes abused. How could you tell if someone was a churchman? A test involving reading a verse from the Bible was often used, because the only educated people were churchmen. However, others learned to recite the test verse from memory – it became known as the 'neck verse' because it could save your neck. People only loosely connected to the Church, such as the door-keeper or the grave-digger used benefit of clergy to escape tougher punishments.

Benefit of clergy was not abolished until 1820.

Church courts

The Church also claimed the right to try moral cases, too: failure to attend church, drunkenness, immorality, playing football on Sundays. See Source 1.

Sanctuary

Someone on the run from the law could not be arrested if he or she took refuge in a church. For some churches this right of sanctuary could be claimed just by seizing the knocker, like the one in Source 2.

The fugitive was then dealt with by the Church, which usually meant being banished from the country. Wearing sack-cloth, barefoot, bare-headed, with an 'A' (for 'abjured') branded on their thumb, they walked to the nearest port.

The right of sanctuary ended with the Reformation in the 16th century.

Source 2

◀ The sanctuary knocker at Durham Cathedral

Quarrels with the king

Monarchs who wanted to extend and enforce royal justice on everyone throughout their realms resented all the Church's interference in their justice. It undermined their power. Several kings and archbishops squabbled over it, but the quarrel came to a head in 1170, when four knights in the service of King Henry II murdered the Archbishop of Canterbury, Thomas Becket, in his cathedral. It is, however, an indication of the power of the Church that Henry was forced to seek forgiveness by lying on the floor in front of Becket's tomb, being whipped by all the priests and monks of Canterbury.

Source 1

From the court of the Archbishop of Canterbury
- Elias, a priest, keeps a certain Agatha in his house for immoral purposes. He is sentenced to be flogged three times around the church.
- Alexander Overy does not attend his parish church when he should. He swears that he will come in future.
- Hamo Corbyl has committed adultery with Basilea Forne. He also behaves badly towards his wife. She appeared and they were reconciled and agree to live together upon pain of seven floggings in the market. Hamo and Basilea were also flogged five times around Romney market.

Activity

Was the Church's influence on justice a good thing? Use a table like this one to summarise your views:

	Good	Bad
Ordeal		
Benefit of clergy		
Church courts		
Sanctuary		

Crime and punishment in Islamic societies

Religion also played a big part in justice in Islamic countries – and still does. Islam makes no distinction between religion and the rest of life: all life is spiritual.

Law

Islamic law, *shari'ah*, is based on the *Qur'an*, the Holy Book of Islam, which consists of messages direct from God as revealed to the Prophet Muhammad. Shari'ah laws are therefore Holy Laws, applying to everyone, at all times. Breaking shari'ah law is therefore not only a crime, but a sin. It covers, for example, family life, education, dress, business, government and hospitality. Source 1 shows how the Qur'an puts all kinds of wrong behaviour together.

> ### Source 1
>
> From the Qur'an
> Liquor and gambling, idols and using divining arrows are only a filthy work of Satan: give them up so you may prosper.

Decisions on shari'ah law are made by *qadi*, judges. They are scholars who have a deep knowledge not only of the Qur'an, but of judgements made by qadis in the past – see Source 3.

Source 2

▲ A medieval illustration of a qadi hearing a case

Source 3

From a book of shari'ah law written in about 1315 by Ibn Taymiyya
A man may be punished for perjury by having his face blackened and being paraded through the streets mounted backwards on a donkey. It is related that Umar ibn-Khattab, may God be pleased with him, used this punishment for a false witness. Because the liar blackened a reputation, his face was blackened. Because he turned words backwards, he was mounted backwards.

Punishment

Shari'ah law is clear: the purposes of punishment are to teach the offender a lesson, to deter others and to give the victim of the crime some revenge. The punishment is chosen to be appropriate, as Source 3 shows. Source 4 is more controversial.

It is important to see shari'ah punishments like these in the light of the situation in 7th century Arabia, when Muhammad was alive. In his time, crimes were often settled by the injured family, which led to feuds that went on for years. In that context, law based on a simple, known punishment is a limitation on vengeance. That is why the punishments are often called *hudud*, which means 'limitation'. The victim's family was always consulted, to see what kind of punishment was considered appropriate.

Shari'ah law also had another role. As the map in Source 5 shows, Islam spread very rapidly in the 120 years after Muhammad's death. Its followers soon stretched from the Atlantic coast to India and from the French border to the Sahara Desert. Many different peoples became Muslims, but shari'ah was the law they all lived by.

Source 4

From the Qur'an

As for the thief, both man and woman, chop off their hands. It is the reward for their own deeds and an exemplary punishment from God.

Activity

Discuss

This section is headed: 'Was justice in the Middle Ages bloody and thoughtless?' Do you think that religion made justice in the Middle Ages less bloody and thoughtless? Use examples from the Christian church as well as examples from the Muslim world to support your answer.

Source 5

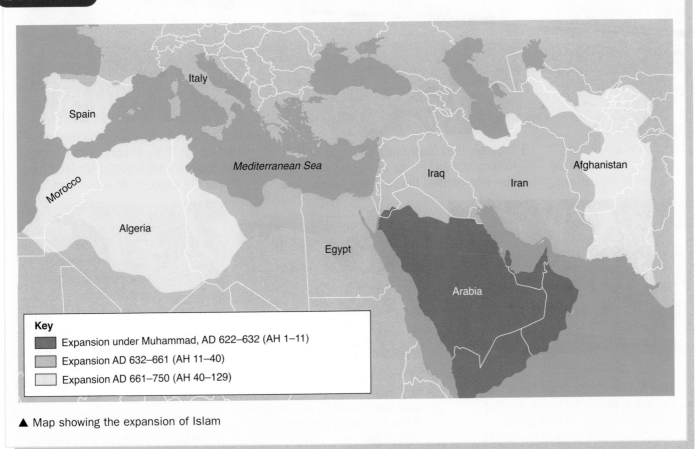

Key
- Expansion under Muhammad, AD 622–632 (AH 1–11)
- Expansion AD 632–661 (AH 11–40)
- Expansion AD 661–750 (AH 40–129)

▲ Map showing the expansion of Islam

3.5 What does the popularity of the Robin Hood story tell us about attitudes to the law in the Middle Ages?

The Story of Robin Hood

1 Robin was the son of a nobleman. He went to the Crusades with King Richard I.

2 Robin returned to find he had lost his lands to the evil Sheriff of Nottingham and Richard's brother, John, was trying to take over the throne.

3 Robin joined a band of outlaws living in Sherwood Forest. The other outlaws were a mix of townspeople, peasants and priests. They had become outlaws because they had been unjustly accused of crimes.

4 Robin was a brilliant archer. He became the leader of the outlaws.

5 Together they fought against the Sheriff of Nottingham and Prince John, and anyone else who harmed the poor and defenceless.

6 If the outlaws stole anything they gave it to the poor. They attacked rich bishops and some priests who did not lead the simple life expected of churchmen.

7 The outlaws were good friends who stayed together for years, sharing everything. They did not suffer hardships from living in the forest.

It is good to be back in England.

8 Eventually King Richard returned from the Crusades, and rewarded Robin for supporting him against King John.

Arise, Sir Robin. All your lands are returned to you.

9 The King gave Robin his lands back.

▲ A 17th century Robin Hood

▲ A Hollywood Robin Hood, 1938

Robin Hood has been the subject of no less than 14 films and several TV series, but he has been a popular figure since the Middle Ages. One of the first books printed in England in 1492 was *A Mery Gest of Robyn Hoode*, but there are references to plays and songs about him long before that. Historians have tried to discover if there was a real Robin Hood, but so far their searches through the records have failed to find him. So he seems to be a legend, a story – or a number of stories. You can read the overall story opposite.

So why was this legendary figure so popular? There must be something about his life and adventures that appealed to medieval people. What can we **infer** from this popularity about ordinary people's views, especially about law and justice?

Whether told round a medieval fireside or on a multiplex cinema screen, here are the features common to most stories about Robin Hood:

- **He was unjustly outlawed.** Medieval justice was not that bad, but it was certainly loaded in favour of the rich and powerful. If you decided to run from justice you would be declared an outlaw and could be killed on sight.

- **He robbed the rich and gave to the poor.** Medieval society was very unequal, with a few living in luxury while most people were desperately poor peasants.

- **His great enemy was the Sheriff of Nottingham.** Sheriffs were royal officials whose job it was to ensure the law was obeyed and make sure taxes were paid, etc.

- **He robbed rich Church leaders.** Some senior officials of the Church – bishops and abbots – lived very well, while village priests were poor.

- **He killed the deer in the forest.** The harsh Forest Laws were hated. Hungry peasants saw deer and other wildlife eating their crops, but were not allowed to kill the animals. Nor were they allowed to collect firewood in the forest.

Activity

Take the five elements of the Robin Hood story (left) one by one.

What can you **infer** about medieval attitudes to the law from the fact that people liked to hear stories about Robin Hood?

Throughout the Middle Ages a king's main duties were to defend his country from enemies and to protect his people from lawbreakers. Between 1100 and 1500, kings took an even closer interest in laws, crimes and punishments. They made important changes to the legal system and this was meant to make the system of catching and punishing criminals more effective. Over the next four pages you will examine these changes through the story of a real medieval murder. So let's start with the crime.

Murder in a medieval village

John the Shepherd's house looked empty. Roger Ryet had already walked past it once, glancing in through the shutter, just out of curiosity. There wasn't much to see – a well-swept floor, a couple of benches, a table. Hanging over the benches was a piece of cloth. 'Nice piece of cloth,' thought Roger, 'it'll make a nice tunic'. He carried on hoping that today he would get work on the lord of the manor's land and then be able to buy a new tunic.

Roger didn't find work. In the village and those all around, there were many men clamouring for work. By the time he arrived, others were already turning away disappointed. Roger cursed, knowing how desperately he needed money. His own scrap of land did not produce enough food to live on.

Now Roger was walking back past John the Shepherd's house again. The shutter still stood open, the cloth still lay on the bench. There was no one nearby. The cloth was within arm's reach through the shutter. Roger reached in, grabbed the cloth and started running.

'Thief!' shouted a man's voice. Roger reeled with shock. Where had the man come from? He had been sure there was no one about.

The man blocked Roger's path, and he could hear a woman running up behind him. Roger hesitated, gripping the cloth tightly. He had to move. He had to run away. In the other hand he held his knife. He moved forward, desperate to escape …

Seconds later, John the Shepherd lay dead. His wife, Isobel, knelt screaming by his side.

Activity

1 This is a true story from Norfolk from the early 1300s. Your task is to decide 'what happened next' after John the Shepherd was killed. Below you can see the possible ways that Roger Ryet may have been caught, put on trial and punished. Only some of them are correct. Predict which statements you think are true and which are false. Keep a note of your predictions. Then read the rest of the reconstructed story that follows. You should be able to work out if your predictions were correct.

 a The local men chased Roger in the hue and cry led by the constable.

 b The Norfolk coroner held an enquiry into the death and the jury decided that there was enough evidence to accuse Roger in court.

 c A message was sent to the local sheriff who took Roger off to prison.

 d When the king's judges arrived in Norfolk, Roger went before the court.

 e Roger faced trial by ordeal, plunging his arm into boiling water.

 f Roger paid Isobel the wergild of 200 shillings for her husband.

 g Roger was hanged by order of the judges.

Escape

'Keep running, don't stop, can't breathe ... must breathe, got to keep on running,' thought Roger. He ran. He didn't know how long for. It seemed like a very long time. His legs should have been aching by now, but surprisingly they felt fine. Looking down he saw the cloth, still gripped tightly in his hand. It was now stained red with John the Shepherd's blood. He stopped to catch his breath in the wood. How had it come to this?

Hue and cry

Roger already knew what would be happening back in the village. Isobel's screams would have raised the hue and cry. Every villager would have downed tools immediately to join in the hunt. No one would risk the fine for not doing so. And they all knew Roger, so it would be easy for them to recognise him.

The constable

Out in the woods Roger stopped for breath, leaning against a large oak tree. He could hear the villagers now. One voice could be heard above the rest. It was Jethro, the constable. Jethro was a blacksmith by trade, but he had volunteered to be the constable for that year. He had respect in the village and people looked up to him. He was just the man for the job. He had to keep the peace in his spare time: keep one eye out for any crime that took place during the night; lead the hue and cry when it was needed. He took his job seriously even though it was unpaid. Roger shivered. His spirits sank. With Jethro leading the hue and cry he felt it was only a matter of time before he was caught.

But Roger was lucky. The hue and cry went the wrong way. He could hear the shouts disappearing in the opposite direction. As Roger relaxed a little he sensed a deep hunger in his belly. If only he hadn't acted in haste, he would be sitting down to his evening meal now.

Activity

2 As you read through the story, on your own copy, underline or highlight in a different colour each part of the story that provides information about the following topics:

Policing   Trials   Punishments

The coroner and the sheriff

Back in the village, food was not a priority for Jethro. He had not found Roger so now he had to tell the coroner about John the Shepherd's death. (Since 1190 all unnatural deaths had to be reported to the coroner.) In this case it was clear what had happened – and the coroner would confirm this with Isobel. The coroner would then have to inform another royal official, the sheriff of the county, that a man had been murdered. And if the hue and cry had still not found Roger then the sheriff's men would send a posse to track down and imprison Roger.

Sanctuary

Out in the woods Roger had a plan. His best hope of escape was to get to the church in nearby Duntown. He would reach the church and bang on the sanctuary door knocker. Once a criminal had reached sanctuary, even the sheriff could not take him by force from a church. Roger would then have the choice of whether to stand trial for his crime or leave the country within 40 days. He'd go to France. Yes, that is what he'd do.

Sleep

Roger moved slowly so no one could hear him – avoiding the country paths; crossing ditches and fields. But this was unfamiliar land now. In the moonless night Roger was well and truly lost. He was back in woodland again, hungry and tired, with regrets flooding his mind. If only ... he'd had enough land to grow food. If only ... he hadn't seen the cloth. If only ... he hadn't used his knife. And there in the wood Roger slowly drifted off to sleep.

Morning

'He's over here! Get up! On your feet!' Roger woke up with a start. Looking up, he saw a finely dressed man, who must be the sheriff, towering above him. There were several men from a nearby village. They had been summoned as part of the sheriff's posse to track down Roger. He recognised one of them as his cousin, a boy of fifteen. Roger didn't blame him; all men of that age could be summoned to join the posse.

It was getting light as they took him away bound with a rope. Roger cursed his luck as he saw the Duntown church on the horizon. It looked so close. He'd have been safe there.

The royal court

Roger was accused of the murder. After a week in the local gaol he was taken, by his tithing, before the royal court. The royal court dealt with the most serious crimes. As he walked in he saw a row of five judges sitting high up. They were dressed in fine red robes. Just below them were some important people writing everything down on large scrolls of paper. To his left Roger could see the jury – he knew them all because they were from his local village. Many of them had heard Isobel's screams as Roger had stabbed John the Shepherd. Isobel stood and gave evidence as an eye witness. Her painful tale lasted less than a minute. The jury trusted her version of events and swore an oath that Roger was guilty. If only she hadn't seen him do it, he might have got away with it! Roger was well liked and trusted by the villagers. Without any evidence they might have sworn an oath of innocence based on his good character. But he had been seen, and the judges quickly declared their sentence …

The noose

'At least I didn't have to go through trial by ordeal,' thought Roger. That had been abolished in 1215. This thought cheered him up for a split second before he remembered his fate. Serious crimes and even some minor crimes like theft were now punished by death. Of course, there were ways of avoiding the death

▲ A medieval illustration of a royal court

penalty. But Roger could not afford to buy a pardon from the king and he wasn't needed to go into the army. He couldn't read, so there was little point in claiming benefit of the clergy. This would have involved him reading a verse from the Bible and being tried by the church courts – they never executed people.

But Roger's fate was sealed. He twitched and convulsed at the end of the hangman's rope.

Activities

1 How many of the statements from page 48 were true? Were your predictions correct?

2 The legal system changed in the later Middle Ages. Copy the table below. Complete it using the information in the story to show what changed.

	Situation in 1100	Changes made by kings	Continuities
Policing	There was no police force. Tithings were organised. Members of the tithing had to bring the accused to court. The hue and cry was used.		
Trials and courts	Juries decided if the accused was guilty. If they couldn't decide then trial by ordeal was used to let God decide. There were royal courts for serious cases and manor courts for others.		
Punishments	The Normans had ended wergild and fines were paid to the king, as his peace had been broken. Serious crimes and re-offenders were punished by death. Those who did not attend court were outlawed.		

3 Which of the statements below do you think best sums up how much the legal system had changed by the later Middle Ages?

a By the end of the Middle Ages justice had changed very little since 1100.

b The key parts of the justice system had been kept since 1100; trials and policing had been improved.

c By the end of the Middle Ages justice had been radically altered. Nearly all aspects of the 1100 system had changed beyond recognition.

> 'From 1100 to 1500 the system of justice changed very little.' Explain how far you agree with this statement. [8]

This exam question is challenging. It tests your knowledge of justice during the later Middle Ages *and* your ability to use this knowledge to **evaluate** change and continuity during the period. It is not simply a case of saying whether you agree or disagree with the statement. Eight marks are available so the examiner will expect you to **explore both sides of the argument**.

Follow the steps below to help you achieve a high grade.

Step 1: The argument for

Look back at the table you produced for the Roger Ryet story (page 51). Select two or three examples that you can use as evidence to prove that there was continuity during this period. You should have more than enough evidence to write a good first paragraph. Selection is important. In the exam you will not have time to write everything down. You should not spend more than 15 minutes answering this type of question.

Try to avoid making general points without fully explaining them and backing them up with a specific example.

Look at the following answer.

> There was a great deal of continuity in the justice system during the later Middle Ages. Punishments were often violent.

The student starts by making a general point. They would score just 1 mark if they stopped here. They are simply saying something, they are not proving anything!

WARNING

Do not stop here

> At the start of the period punishments were often violent. Serious crimes like treason were punished by death. At the end of the period the death penalty was still used. Treason was still punished by death. Harsh punishments were still seen as a deterrent.

However, the student goes on to score extra marks by *proving the point*. The student compares ideas about punishments at the start and the end of the period.

Step 2: The argument against

What evidence could you use from your table to argue against the statement? Select evidence and use it to prove that there was also change during this period. This will help you to form a good second paragraph. Remember to back up the points you make with a good explanation and a specific example.

Step 3: The conclusion

This is a crucial part of your answer. It is usually the part that pupils forget or present poorly. Just producing a balanced answer is not enough. You have been asked to evaluate the extent to which you agree or disagree with the statement. It would be easy to sit on the fence and avoid reaching a final conclusion. Sitting on the fence is a dangerous position. Your answer collapses and you lose marks!

   Instead, you need to be confident and reach an **overall judgement**. Imagine that you could put the evidence on scales. Which way would the scales tip – towards change or towards continuity? Which side has the strongest evidence to support it? Think about the main themes: policing, trials and punishments. Write down your opinion and explain the key reason you have come to your conclusion.

What makes an effective conclusion?

Things to avoid

- A detailed summary of everything that has already been said.
- A one sentence conclusion that reaches an overall judgement but does not explain it or show that there are two sides to the argument.
- A weak conclusion that sits on the fence and does not reach an overall judgement.

Things to do

- Focus on the question. You could use words or phrases from the question in your final paragraph.
- Come to a strong overall judgement.
- Explain your main reason for reaching this judgement.
- Show that you recognise that there is evidence which agrees and disagrees with the statement.

WARNING

Do not sit on the fence

How to structure a conclusion

| Start by conceding that the weaker argument has some strengths. Give an example. | → | Then make it clear that the other argument is stronger. | → | Provide your main piece(s) of evidence that supports this. | → | Try and end with a memorable final sentence. |

For example:

In some ways the later Middle Ages was a period of continuity.

Violent punishments were used throughout the period.

However, overall I disagree. Trial by ordeal was abolished in 1215 and trials became more reliant on evidence. This was a crucial change in the development of trials.

Although tithings were still used, the existing system of self-policing was improved with the introduction of constables and sheriffs.

Women, Crime and Punishment in the Middle Ages

Women were not treated equally with men in the Middle Ages. Anglo-Saxon law gave women the right to own land and to defend themselves in court, but Norman law was much tougher on them. This was because it was based on Church law – see Source 1.

'Subject to the rule of men' in Source 1 meant that a woman had to obey her father when at home, and her husband when she married. These two took over all her rights. A woman could not:

- marry without her father's consent

- divorce her husband

- get custody of her children if her husband divorced her

- own property or goods of any kind, even clothes. This meant that women could not go into business in their own right

- inherit land or money or property from her parents: only sons could do that, not daughters. Widows had the right to just enough land to keep them alive.

There was even a special offence against women who would not accept their role: being a 'scold' – see Source 2.

It is hard for historians to find out about the lives of women in the Middle Ages. They could not take action in the royal law courts, as Source 1 says, so don't appear in the records. However, the manor court, which dealt with ordinary village disputes, gives a different picture. Sources 3 show women playing a lively part in village life.

Source 1

Gratian, an 11th century Church lawyer.

Woman's authority is nil. Let her in all things be subject to the rule of men. She cannot teach, be a witness in court, or sit in judgement.

Source 2

From the records of the City of London, 1375. Alice was sentenced to an hour in the pillory.

Alice Shether was brought before the Mayor for being a scold. All her neighbours were greatly annoyed by her malicious words and abuse. She sowed envy, discord and ill-will, repeatedly defaming and backbiting many of them.

Source 3A

From Colchester Court Rolls, 1310

Isabella Porter should come to court to reply to Matilda Alured on a charge of keeping a sow which killed and ate 14 ducklings belonging to the said Matilda.

Source 3B

From Wakefield Court Rolls, 1294

A jury is summoned to inquire into the case of Hancock le Nunne's sheep. His wife Alicia is accused of saying that the jury were lying and that Adam Gerbot would swear anything for a gallon of ale.

Source 3C

Court Roll, 1267

William of Stansgate met the widow Desiderata, a friend and godmother of his son. She asked him in jest if he was one of the men appointed constable. She declared she could overcome two or three men like him, crooked her leg, grabbed him by the neck and threw him to the ground.

Activity

1 Which of the restrictions on women's rights in the Middle Ages would you find the most difficult to live with?

2 In what ways do the Court Rolls evidence, Sources 3A–C, give a different picture of women's lives?

Activities

Middle Ages summary

1 So far in this chapter you have made a number of revision cards. It is now time to make the final four cards, as below.

Constables

Description

Explanation

Changes

Sheriff and posse

Description

Explanation

Changes

Coroner

Description

Explanation

Changes

Royal courts

Description

Explanation

Changes

Draw an image on the back of each card to help trigger your memory.

2 You have been making revision cards for Saxon and Norman crime, punishment and policing. Now you are going to find out how useful these cards are. They already summarise the information you will need for your exam but they also help you analyse information, which is much more important for getting a good grade than just knowing things.

Step 1: Complete your cards to show what changed

Check each card and decide: *Did this change after the Saxons?* If it did then write a sentence to explain how it changed. If it didn't write: 'No'!

Step 2: Sort the cards

You can do this in various ways.

a Put all of the *continuities* in one group. This means all the things that stayed the same throughout the Middle Ages, for example, the hue and cry.

b Put all of the *changes* made by the Normans in another group, for example, fines payable to the king. How else can you sort these cards?

Step 3: Answer the big question

The cards can also help you to answer the big question that was posed at the beginning of this section: Was justice in the Middle Ages bloody and thoughtless?

a Sort your cards into three groups: policing, trials and punishments.

b Take the punishment cards first and place them on the line below.

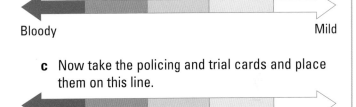

Bloody   Mild

c Now take the policing and trial cards and place them on this line.

Thoughtless   Thoughtful

d Which of the statements below do you think answer the big question the best:

- Justice in the Middle Ages was bloody and thoughtless.
- Justice in the Middle Ages was mild and thoughtless.
- Justice in the Middle Ages was mild and thoughtful.
- Justice in the Middle Ages was bloody and thoughtful.

Be prepared to back up your answer with at least three examples.

smarter revision tips

Now you have sorted your cards on to the two lines it is a good idea to play the What? and Why? game (see page 38) for the whole of the Middle Ages.

Now you know how to make **revision cards**, and different ways of using them, you can make and use them to revise other topics in this course.

The Middle Ages covers a long period of time. A **timeline** helps you to summarise *when* things happened, and how everything that happened *fits together*. See page 11 for how to make and use a timeline.

Section 4: Crime and punishment in the Early Modern Period, 1500–1750

You might know the Early Modern Period as the time that includes the Tudors and Stuarts, famous for Henry VIII, Charles I, the English Civil War and Oliver Cromwell. As you know from your work at Key Stage 3, there was a change in attitudes during this period: England became a Protestant country. Rich landowners in Parliament wanted a say in the making of laws. This became such a big issue that Parliament went to war with the King in 1642, and executed him in 1649! In 1688, when William and Mary came over from Holland to rule the country, Parliament made sure they had the power to make laws. How would you expect all these changes to affect crime, punishment, trials and policing? These pages should help you to find out.

Criminal moment in time 3: Portsmouth 1732

Watchmen were employed in towns to patrol the streets both day and night. But they were poorly paid and of little use.

Poaching was a serious crime punishable by death.

Your money or your life.

Look, there is a £1 reward if we catch Richard Turnip, the famous highway robber.

Then let's go and look for him.

1534 Henry VIII set up the Church of England

1542 First law against witchcraft

1605 The Gunpowder Plot

1500   1550   1600

E A R L Y   M O D E R N

Over 150 crimes were punishable by death.

You can't seem to do anything today without facing the death penalty. I've heard that cutting down trees, stealing rabbits, stealing sheep and lots of other crimes are punished by death.

I'm here because I'm in debt, but I can't earn any money in prison to pay them.

I'm only in this 'prison' until my trial – thank God.

Smuggling goods such as tea, coffee and sugar was a serious crime, punished by death. But most people dealt in smuggled goods and resented this law.

Justices of the Peace (magistrates) dealt with minor crimes. At the Quarter Sessions, held four times a year, travelling royal judges dealt with more serious crimes. Trials were short – often less than an hour. All cases were decided by a jury.

I've shouted stop thief but only a few people have started to look for him. I don't know, things are not like they used to be! I've got no chance of catching the thief myself in this busy town!

COURT HOUSE

BAKER   FINE CLOTH

1642–49
The English
Civil War

1650

1688
Glorious
Revolution

1700

1715
The Riot
Act

1718
Transportation
Act

1723
The Black Act
increased the
number of capital
offences by 50

1736
Last law against
witchcraft repealed

1750

P E R I O D

4.1 The Big Story – why did punishments become so harsh in the Early Modern Period?

As you read on the pages 56–57, the Early Modern Period was the beginning of the big shift in power and politics from the monarch to rich landowners in Parliament. In 1688 these rich landowners made sure they had the power to make laws. You might think that these men would be more open minded than kings when it came to making laws about punishments. But were they?

Source 1

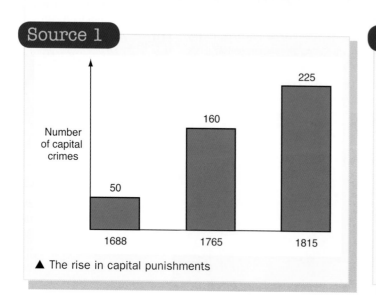

▲ The rise in capital punishments

Source 2

Some of the crimes that carried the death penalty in the 1700s:

Stealing horses or sheep
Destroying turnpike roads
Cutting down growing trees
Pick-pocketing goods worth one shilling [5p] or more
Shop-lifting goods worth five shillings [25p] or more
Being out at night with a blackened face
Sending threatening letters
Deliberately breaking tools used to manufacture wool
Stealing from a rabbit warren
Murder
(plus over 150 more)

Look at Sources 1 and 2. Do you notice the big change?

The big change is that the number of apparently minor crimes punishable by death rose gradually from the late 1600s throughout the 1700s. On occasions this happened really quickly – in 1723, 50 new capital crimes were added – but overall this **Bloody Code** is what we call a trend, i.e. it happened gradually over a relatively long period of time.

But why did it happen? This is where those friendly factors that you met on pages 4–5 can be really helpful.

Activities

Here are the nine factors that you met at the beginning of this book.

1 Read the information on the opposite page. Discuss which factors helped increase the number of capital offences.

2 Discuss how each factor may have helped bring about the Bloody Code.

The MPs who passed the laws that made up the Bloody Code were **wealthy landowners**. Their motives for passing those laws were a mixture of wanting to do good for the people as a whole and wanting to defend their own rights. They also owned property and wanted to **protect their property** from thieves and others who they regarded as criminals.

The patterns of crime hadn't changed since the Middle Ages – most crime was theft of low value items: money, food and belongings. But some crimes that had existed for a long time became very well known in this period because they were publicised in pamphlets and broadsheets that had not existed in the Middle Ages. Generally, only the very wealthy or clergy could read and these men were now in Parliament making laws about crimes and punishments.

A number of crimes became common during this period. Vagabonds or tramps begged for food, highwaymen held up coaches and stole money, poachers hunted food from other people's land and smugglers brought goods like tea and rum into the country to avoid paying taxes on them. These goods were then distributed around the country and sold illegally. The **'new' crimes** emerged because **travel became easier**. Restrictions were lifted and more people were able to move around.

Some people were getting richer. But **many of the population were very poor**. In hard times, when the harvest failed or the economy was doing badly, the poor had nothing to fall back on yet they needed food and clothes to survive. Some stole what they needed.

Heresy – how did religion influence crime and punishment in this period?

So you think religious fanaticism, attempted assassination, martyrdom and the use of torture to obtain evidence only happen in the 21st century? Read on!

Rulers in the 16th and 17th centuries expected their subjects to practise the same religion as they did. This could make for difficulties when, as in 16th century England, the religion of the ruler kept changing. If you did not practise the same religion as the ruler you were called a **heretic**. The normal punishment for heresy was death by burning.

Source 1

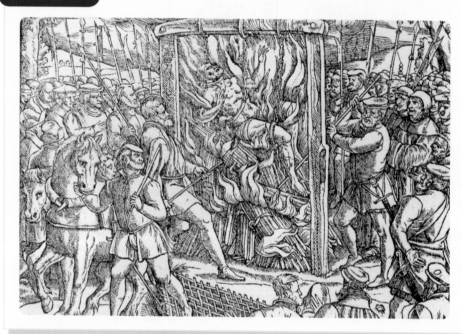

◀ A heretic being burned in the 15th century. Heretics were burned so their bodies were utterly destroyed, leaving nothing for the day when, Christians believe, God will resurrect all true believers.

In the early 16th century there was only one Church in England: the Roman Catholic Church. Then, in the 1530s, Henry VIII broke with Rome, and England became a Protestant country. Henry's son Edward VI continued with this religious policy, but when he died in 1553 Henry's eldest daughter, Mary, became queen. Mary was determined to restore the Roman Catholic faith in England. Some 280 men and women were arrested as heretics. They were tried and, if they refused to change their beliefs, burned. Some had been important bishops in Henry's reign, but most were ordinary people, prepared to die for their beliefs.

Mary died in 1558 and was succeeded by her half-sister, Queen Elizabeth I. Elizabeth was quite tolerant of religious differences. She said she 'would not make a window into men's souls'. But in 1570 the Pope declared her to be a heretic and released all Roman Catholics in England from having to obey her.

This was serious. It meant that Elizabeth could be assassinated – William of Orange, leader of the Netherlands, was assassinated in 1584. It also gave the strongly Roman Catholic King Philip of Spain a reason to invade England and overthrow Elizabeth, which he attempted to do in 1588 with his Armada.

The government therefore regarded Roman Catholic priests not as heretics, but as traitors. The punishment for treason was, if anything, even more horrific than burning. The condemned traitor was **hanged, drawn** and **quartered**. That is, they were hanged by the neck until almost dead, then they were cut open and had their genitals and innards burned before them. Finally, the body was beheaded and cut into four parts. The head and the four quarters were publicly displayed in various parts of the country.

Activities

1 What factors can you identify that help explain why heresy was seen as a serious crime?

2 Discuss how each factor helped make heresy a crime.

The Gunpowder Plot, 1605

Elizabeth died in 1603 and was succeeded by King James I. A group of fanatical Roman Catholics decided to assassinate James and all his ministers when they arrived to open Parliament. An explosives expert, Guy Fawkes, prepared 36 barrels of gunpowder in a cellar underneath the House of Lords. On the evening of 5 November 1605, the cellars were searched and Guy Fawkes was arrested. He was tortured on the rack and revealed the names of his fellow conspirators. Eight of the leaders were hanged, drawn and quartered.

Source 2

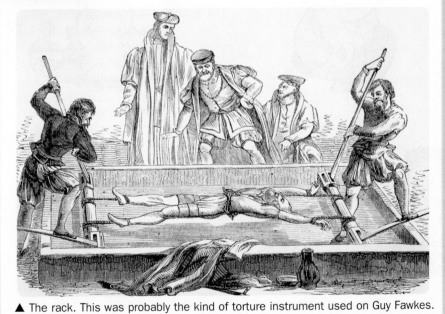

▲ The rack. This was probably the kind of torture instrument used on Guy Fawkes.

Source 3

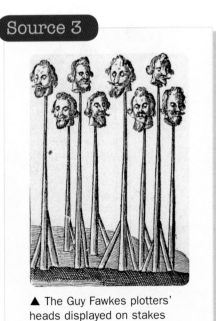

▲ The Guy Fawkes plotters' heads displayed on stakes

61

4.2 Why were there so many 'new' crimes in the Early Modern Period?

People became increasingly worried about certain crimes during this time period – so much so that the punishment for many crimes was death by execution. We are going to focus on four of these crimes and work out why each one developed. Our friendly factors are important here. If you can remember the factors you should be able to answer a whole host of 'explain' questions, which often appear in the exam.

Activity

1 Which factor was most influential in causing the new crimes? If you look at the factors below you will see that they are all arguing! As you work through this section you will become one of these factors and try to work out if you can be the 'criminal mastermind'.

I am the true criminal mastermind because I made people so desperate that they were willing to commit crimes.

No, I am the true criminal mastermind! People have always hated me. They broke the law and smuggled goods into the country to avoid paying taxes. Without me, smuggling would never have become a crime.

You're all wrong – I am the true criminal mastermind. Without me, no laws would have been passed to make all of these things crimes in the first place!

POVERTY AND WEALTH

TAXES

GOVERNMENT AND LAWMAKERS

TRAVEL

MEDIA

It was me. It was all because people started travelling all over the place. There's nothing better than travel for stirring things up.

In the end you will all see the truth. It was media that did it. Without the broadsheets and the books, no one would have heard of these crimes so they wouldn't have been worried, and so …

Activity

2 Work in small groups. These are the **five** key factors affecting crime in this period. You are going to represent one of them:

GOVERNMENT AND LAWMAKERS

TRAVEL

TAXES

MEDIA

POVERTY AND WEALTH

Your task is to gather convincing evidence to prove that your factor was the most influential in the growth of the four new crimes that you are going to study over the next eight pages. You need to decide how important your factor was in bringing about each crime and give it a rating between 1 (very important) and 5 (not important).

Record your evidence in a factor table or a spreadsheet, like the one below.

(Factor): e.g. Travel	
Crime	
Evidence of factor's impact	
Rating	
Justification of rating	

New Crime 1: Vagrancy – why did vagrancy become a serious crime in the 16th century?

Walk through any town or city today and you are likely to come across homeless people selling the *Big Issue* or begging. This is a sad state of affairs. Many people buy the *Big Issue* to help the homeless. Those caught begging are often not punished. In the 16th and 17th centuries, monarchs and law makers had a very different attitude towards what they called 'vagrants' and 'vagabonds'.

Vagabonds were actually beggars, tramps and vagrants who wandered around the country without a settled job. Some of them were demobbed soldiers, others were criminals, but most were unemployed people moving to a new town looking for work.

It is difficult to know how many vagabonds and vagrants were actually executed.

Source 1

Many idle vagabonds and other lewd and rebellious persons, showing no fear of God and forgetting their duty of allegiance to us, do still loiter and use rebellious and stubborn talk, refusing to do work …

You shall cause our Justices of the Peace and our other ministers, officers and good subjects of that county, to find those who are spreading seditious tales and rumours, or raising outcries, ringing bells, sounding trumpets or drums, or using any other ways to raise the people or gather any meetings which have not been ordered by us. When they appear, you shall forthwith arrest them as rebels and open traitors to us and our realm, and they are to be, without delay, hanged and executed openly to the terror of others.

Vagabonds or idle persons refusing to work are to be similarly arrested and punished.

▲ An extract from a draft of a letter (dated 1549) from Edward VI to the Justices of the Peace and Sheriffs in counties where there had been unrest (rebellions)

Activities

1 On your own copy of Source 1, underline in the first paragraph what vagabonds were doing wrong.

2 King Edward VI was clearly worried about rebels as well as vagabonds. Highlight how he states both should be punished.

3 The letter is an example of the influence of government and law makers on crimes. For those of you representing the Government and Law Makers factor, the first part of the table has been completed for you. You need to come up with a rating and a justification for your rating.

4 For those of you representing the other factors, you need to read file cards A–E on the next page and start your own table.

Government and Law Makers	
Crime	Vagrancy
Evidence of factor's impact	Edward VI ordered his Justices of the Peace to punish vagabonds by being executed in public. This is an example of a monarch making a law. If Edward hadn't passed this law, vagrants or vagabonds might not have been classed as criminals.
Rating	
Justification of rating	

From the late 15th century, the invention of printing meant that books were published on many topics. This book by Thomas Harman described how terrible vagabonds were. He wrote, '*They are all thieves and extortioners. They lick the sweat from the true labourers brow and take from the Godly poor what is due to them.*' Books and pamphlets like these were used to increase people's fear of vagrancy. But generally only wealthy landowners and law makers could read so the vast majority of ordinary people would not have seen Harman's work.

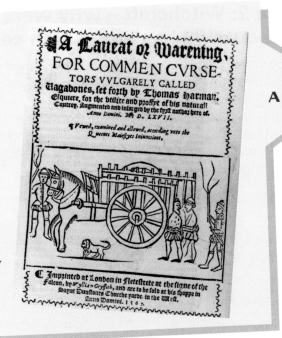

A

Some vagabonds were undoubtedly criminals – cutpurses, petty thieves and fraudulent beggars – as described by Thomas Harman. But most vagabonds were not criminals or devious beggars. They were genuinely poor, unemployed people looking for work. As the population grew there simply wasn't enough work. In years of good harvests people could only just get by. When the harvests failed and bread prices rose the poor became desperate. Some were forced to beg for food.

B

Each village and town did try to help the poor in their own area. The old, sick and poor received help to buy food from the poor rate – a tax paid for by the richer people in the village. This system worked fairly well in the Middle Ages because people didn't really travel. By the 1500s this had changed. Restrictions on travel had been removed and more people were travelling from town to town. This meant those in one village were having to pay for the travelling poor as well as 'their own' poor. Some didn't like this.

C

When Edward VI came to the throne in 1547, Protestant advisers encouraged Puritan ideas. Puritan religion taught that everyone should work hard so they wouldn't be tempted to commit sins. In fact, not working was seen as a crime and a sin in its own right. Many people adopted these new ideas. But many people remained Catholic.

D

London grew dramatically in the 17th century. It was by far the largest city in Europe. The population rose tenfold in just over 150 years from 50,000 in 1500 to 500,000 in 1665. Many people went there looking for work or good opportunities for crime. Even so, in 1560 the London 'Bridwell' or house of correction dealt with only 69 vagabonds.

E

Activity

5 Discuss what other factors, apart from Government and Law Makers, Travel, Taxes, Media and Poverty and Wealth, are mentioned here. How important do you think these factors are?

New Crime 2: Witchcraft – why were people so worried about witches in the 17th century?

Over the last 50 years, Halloween night has become something of a celebration. Children dress as witches and goblins; they go out 'trick or treating' and enjoy themselves in an imagined world of witchcraft. But 400 years ago this world wasn't imagined, it was deadly serious. After 1542, the punishment for being a witch was execution, and roughly a thousand people, mainly women, were found guilty of witchcraft and punished in this way between 1542 and 1715.

Source 1

Margaret Johnson, widow, aged 60 years or thereabouts, said that she has been a witch about six years. This happened after she had some troubles and arguments with her neighbours. After one argument she went walking in the highway in Marsden in the parish of Whalley, there appeared to her a Man in black attire who said to her: If she would give him her soul, she should want for nothing, but should have power to hurt whom she liked both man and beast. She then refused and thereupon he vanished. In this manner he often times came to her, till at last she yielded [gave in] to him, and he gave her into her hand some silver and gold (as she thought) but it vanished soon again, and she knows not how. And she asked his name and he called himself Mamilion ... And after this he appeared to her in other shapes: as sometimes of a brown coloured Dog; sometimes of a white Cat, and at other times like an hare; and that these did suck her blood in her privie parts; one wherof is as big (so she said) as her little Finger, and half as long; the other less: But since she lay in prison they have shrunk up and grown less than formerly.

▲ An extract from a letter dated 15 June 1634 from the Bishop of Chester to the Right Honourable Sir John Cooke, and Sir Francis Windebank, Knights, Principal Secretaries to King Charles I.

In the Middle Ages witchcraft was regarded as a minor crime and was dealt with by the church courts. Between 1066 and 1500 only a handful of witches were hanged. But in 1542, Parliament passed a law that said witchcraft was a crime punishable by death. In 1604, another even harsher law was passed by James I and his Parliament. Anyone shown to have contacted evil spirits could be hanged, whether they had done any harm or not.

A

Activities

1 As you will know from your study of history at Key Stage 3, it is really important to understand the context of a source. Who was this letter sent from and who was it sent to?

2 Read the letter – what things do you find difficult to believe actually happened in this case? Underline them on your own copy.

3 Margaret Johnson's confession isn't reliable (sorry to disappoint you but people didn't have witch-like powers, even nearly 400 years ago), but it reveals a lot to us about the Church's and the government's attitude towards witches. What was their attitude? Explain your answer.

4 Those of you representing the Government and Law Makers, use your answer to question 3 to help complete your table. You can add more information by reading file cards A–G.

5 For those of you representing the other factors, you also need to read file cards A–G to find evidence for your own factor and then fill in your tables.

One individual, Matthew Hopkins, was responsible for hundreds of women confessing and being executed for witchcraft in Essex in 1645. For reasons unknown, Hopkins scoured East Anglia for witches. In Manningtree he named 36 women as witches and gathered evidence against them. He tortured his suspects by forcing them to stand, and starving them of sleep. Worn down, many confessed. Hopkins also claimed that he had seen their 'familiars'. If a mouse or spider found its way into the cell he claimed it was created by the devil. He also found 'the devil's marks' on witches' bodies. Nineteen of the 36 suspects were executed, and nine more died in gaol.

B

Alice Smith, a 76-year-old woman, was charged (together with her husband and daughter) with causing the illness of a ten-year-old girl. Alice, her husband and daughter were all executed. Stories like these were published as pamphlets and they increased people's fear of witchcraft. Only the very wealthy landowners and law makers could read, so pamphleteers included pictures, which showed executions.

C

This was a time of massive religious change. Puritans and other Protestants preached that the devil and his servants were trying to draw good Christians away from God. Monarchs like James I were strongly religious. James I was influenced by his Puritan ministers to pass the 1604 law (see file card A). There were many more witchcraft trials in Essex than in other areas. This might be because Essex was a strongly Puritan area.

D

By the 1500s, travel was easier. More people were travelling the country looking for work. They sometimes brought with them stories they had heard about witches and this increased people's fears. Matthew Hopkins travelled across Essex and East Anglia (see file card B).

E

There seems to have been more witchcraft trials in years when people were living through times of great hardship and poverty. In the 1580s, a time of poor harvests, the number of witchcraft trials went up dramatically. When people were desperate and hungry they were more likely to accuse their neighbours of causing harm or even wrecking the harvest. But in times of peace and plenty there were far fewer trials.

F

There seems to be little evidence that taxation played a major role in bringing about witchcraft. In times of desperation, taxes may have made some people even worse off.

G

6 Discuss what other factors, apart from Government and Law Makers, Travel, Taxes, Media and Poverty and Wealth, are mentioned here. How important do you think these factors are?

Activity

6 Discuss what other factors, apart from Government and Law Makers, Travel, Taxes, Media and Poverty and Wealth, are mentioned here. How important do you think these factors are?

New Crime 3: Highway robbery – why did highway robbery become such a serious crime?

Source 1 is the front cover of a magazine published in 1905. It turned the story of the famous highway robber, Dick Turpin, into an adventure. In this particular story Turpin tries to reassure a young woman while he holds up and robs a stagecoach. It was actually Turpin and his accomplice who were the criminals or 'villains' here, although the comic suggests they were the heroes.

Highway robbery became a greatly feared crime in the late 17th and early 18th centuries. This was the crime of using force to steal money or property from travellers. But today, thanks partly to the legend of Dick Turpin, we believe that highway robbers were gentlemen who were polite to their victims, especially women. This legend of Dick Turpin developed long after his death. A poem published in 1825 made Turpin the most famous highwayman of all time.

Activities

1 What questions do you have about Source 1?

2 Which of these words would you use to describe the two men on horseback in this picture:

dashing brutal ruthless handsome scruffy fashionable common gentlemanly heroic mysterious frightening romantic murderous?

3 Now read the text below to see if you can answer your questions.

4 What words from the list above would you use to describe the reality of highway robbers?

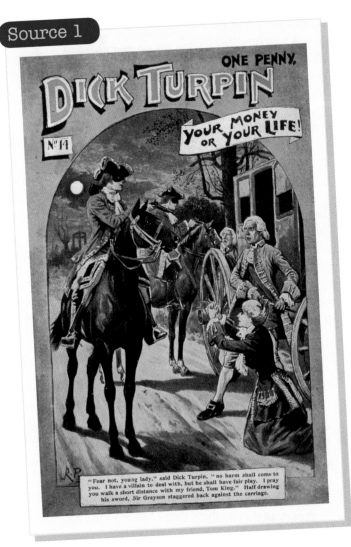

Source 1

"Fear not, young lady," said Dick Turpin, "no harm shall come to you. I have a villain to deal with, but he shall have fair play. I pray you walk a short distance with my friend, Tom King." Half drawing his sword, Sir Grayson staggered back against the carriage.

He was supposed to have escaped the law by riding his horse, Black Bess, from London to York in just one day.

However, the reality of highway robbery is quite different to the legend. Many highway robbers were treacherous, cruel and violent. One highwayman's mask slipped during a robbery and he was recognised by a woman. He cut out her tongue to stop her reporting him. Highway robbers were greatly feared by travellers and they were seen as a major danger to traders and businessmen, especially in London, because they disrupted trade.

The real Dick Turpin was very different to the Dick Turpin portrayed in the comic. He was a ruthless, violent criminal. He was born in Essex in 1705 and was trained as a butcher. He soon turned to cattle stealing. He joined a gang of house breakers who violently threatened their victims. When some of the gang were arrested and hanged, Turpin, along with a friend called Tom King, took up highway robbery. They lived in a cave in Epping Forest. Turpin was ruthless. He robbed lone women travellers and murdered at least one man who tried to capture him. He may well have murdered Tom King when they were both cornered in 1737: King died from a shot from Turpin's gun. Turpin then fled to Yorkshire and took up horse stealing. He was hanged in 1739. He never owned a horse called Black Bess, nor did he ride from London to York in a day. But people have been influenced by the power of the media. Source 1 is a good example.

5 Here are our five key factors. The statements A–H explain the rise of highway robbery. Work out which statements are examples of which factors. Be careful as some of them can be used as examples of more than one factor.

MEDIA

A Books and pamphlets were commonly published in the early 18th century. According to Lucy Moore, an historian, 'For the first time, printing was cheap enough to reach the masses, and literacy rates were increasing.' People enjoyed reading about the adventures of highway robbers.

B One book that highlighted the rise of highway robbery was published by a Captain Smith in 1714. It was called *The General History of the Lives of the … Highwaymen.*

GOVERNMENT AND LAWMAKERS

C Horses were cheaper to buy at this time.

D The number of roads around London greatly increased and stagecoach services increased.

E Ex-soldiers who came home from fighting in the army found themselves without work and became desperate for money.

TAXES

F Luxury goods like tea and brandy were taxed by the government during this period.

POVERTY AND WEALTH

TRAVEL

G Rich merchants were travelling around England in coaches carrying large amounts of money with which to conduct business.

H The government became so worried about highway robbery that it was made a capital offence.

6 Read this sentence: **This could suggest that people wanted more money to buy luxury goods and may have resulted in a few people becoming highway robbers.** This is an explanatory sentence for taxes. Those of you representing taxes can use this in your table. Remember to give taxes a rating.

7 Those of you representing the other factors need to fill in your chart using the statements on this page.

Remember to explain how important your factor was in making highway robbery a crime and to give your factor a rating.

8 What other factors, apart from Poverty and Wealth, Media, Taxes and Government and Law Makers, are mentioned here? Are they more or less important than the factors listed?

New Crime 4: Smuggling – did everyone in the 18th century agree that smuggling was a serious crime?

Smuggling is the crime of bringing goods into the country without paying tax on them. During the 18th century, smuggling became a serious crime – it was punishable by death. But did everyone think that it was a terrible crime?

Source 1

We beg leave to acquaint your Honours that on the 1st Instant, Mr Edward Skeat one of the Landwaiters at this Port, who proceeded with the Collectors and several other officers of Excise, who had received an Information against Captain Gwyn of his Majesty's Ship Ambuscade, of having run on Shore and convey'd to his house at Upham near Waltham, a large Quantity of Brandy, Rum, Arrack and Wine, agreable to which Information they immediately proceeded and found in the house of said Captain Gwyn the following particulars, Viz. five Casks two Hampers containing Brandy, four Casks Rum, Eleven large Bottles Arrack, One hogshead of Spanish, three half Hogsheads and one Pipe of Lisbon Wine, and one hogshead, three hampers of Claret, all which Liquors the Officers would have brought away with them, but were …'

▲ This letter is from the senior Customs officials at Portsmouth in 1748. It describes what happened when customs officers went to investigate a Captain Gwyn, a Naval officer, suspected of possessing smuggled goods. There is a transcript alongside.

Activity

1 Read the text above, which is the beginning of the letter in Source 1, and discuss the following questions.

- Who did the 'excise officers' (customs officers) think was smuggling goods?
- What different goods were found at the house?
- What does this source suggest about the government's attitude to smuggling? Explain your answer.
- This is only the first half of the letter – do you think that the customs officers managed to take away the smuggled goods?

... Obstructed by a Number of People assembled, not less than thirty, amongst the Mob was Captain Gwyn frequently, and as fast as the Officers endeavoured to bring the said Liquors Away, the same was taken from them by the Country People, therefore whatever the Officers endeavored to do, proving ineffectual, at last were Obliged to leave behind them the Said Liquors.

Information

Key words
Endeavoured – tried hard
Liquors – different types of alcohol
Ineffectual – not effective

Activities

2 Read the rest of the letter, above. Discuss what actually happened.
   • What does this suggest about people's attitudes to smuggling? Explain your answer.
   • Why do you think that the law makers and the people disagreed about smuggling being a crime?
3 Those of you representing the Government and Law Makers, use the letter to fill in your table for smuggling.
4 Those of you representing the other factors, read below to find evidence to fill in your table for smuggling.

During the 18th century, the government increased taxes on imported goods to raise extra money. These taxes were really unpopular because they raised the price of many luxury goods and made them expensive: let's face it, people have always liked a little luxury! A massive black market was established. Instead of paying the tax on goods like tea, sugar and brandy, they were smuggled into the country and sold to people for a cheaper price. The punishment for smuggling was, of course, death.

In 1748, 103 people were listed as being wanted for smuggling. Over 70 per cent of them were poor labourers. For farm labourers, smuggling was a quicker way of making money. In a single night, a smuggler could earn six or seven times a farm labourer's wage. Those who helped transport the goods from ship to shore could earn twice as much as a labourer. In Sussex, some smugglers came from the cloth industry which was declining in the 1700s; others who lost their jobs in the fishing and iron-making industries turned to smuggling. For the poor, smuggling was a good way to make a living in good times and bad.

Smuggling gangs were very well organised. They used the major improvements in transport to help them. Goods were smuggled in on all kinds of ships and boats – often in the middle of the night. Smugglers from Sussex, on the south-east coast, could transport their goods from the coast straight to London using the improved road system. They might sell between 1,000 and 2,000 lbs of tea to dealers in one night.

The government was so worried about smuggling that it actually produced wanted posters. This had little effect as people saw the posters as advertising and, because they hated paying tax on imported goods, they were encouraged to support smuggling even more. So the influence of this form of media didn't help the government. It actually encouraged people to smuggle.

▲ An engraving of smugglers breaking open the King's Custom House at Poole

The five factors have all been busy trying to prove that they were the criminal mastermind – the most important factor in bringing about Early Modern crimes. In fact, they have been so busy being selfish and competitive that they have forgotten that working together is really important: in history, things don't happen for just one reason. We are going to build a concept map to illustrate how factors combine together to influence change.

Using a concept map

The students on the opposite page are building a concept map. Concept maps help you develop good explanations. They will:

- help you identify which factors explain why the different crimes happened
- show you how the factors worked together (the green ropes the students are using)
- show you which factor was the most important (the 'criminal mastermind').

You can do them on paper or as a physical map, as on page 73, using tabards and ropes.

Activities

1 On your concept map, put one of the five new Early Modern crimes in the centre – we have started with vagrancy. Decide which factors connect with this crime (the red ropes).

2 As you can see we have added the links (green ropes) – that is how the different factors link together to cause the crime. The green boxes (right) help explain how some of these factors combined. Match each green box with a link.

3 Unfortunately, someone has stolen the rest of the links and explanations (there are criminals everywhere!). Think of your own explanation to match your green and red links.

4 Can you link some of the other factors sitting around the edge? Remember, you must be able to link each one to another factor and explain how they worked together to cause vagrancy.

5 Finally, crown the factor that you think was the criminal mastermind (the most important factor) for vagrancy.

6 Repeat this process for as many crimes as you dare!

> Poor people, desperate because of poverty, were forced to travel to look for work in another area. Instead they often found resentment from the locals who didn't want to provide money to support them.

> The rich people in a parish did not want to pay taxes to support vagrants who had appeared in their village or town, as well as the poor who already lived there.

Your **Historical Source Investigation** exam is an enquiry into a historical topic, based on a group of sources. You will have one and a half hours to answer six questions on these sources.

You will need to use your knowledge of the topic and the background information supplied to help you interpret and evaluate the sources and reach conclusions.

THE WITCH CRAZE

Background information

The 'Witch craze', as it has been called, is an example of a 'crime' which hardly existed until it was created by the government. It was enforced for a while, and then fell into disuse. It lasted from the middle of the 16th century to the early 18th century. During that time, hundreds of people were arrested on suspicion of being a witch. They were interrogated, suffered what amounted to torture, and many were executed. Many more died in prison as a result of their treatment. Witchcraft ceased to be a crime in 1736. What did people believe that allowed this to happen? Did everyone believe in witches?

Source A *King James explains why he wrote his book on witchcraft, published in 1597:*

'There are so many at this time and in this country of these detestable slaves of the devil, the witches, that it has encouraged me to write this book so I can convince the doubting hearts of any that such attacks by Satan are practised.'

Source B *Agnes Waterhouse's confession to being a witch, 1569. She was executed.*

Then said the Judge: 'When did your cat suck your blood?' 'Never', said she. 'No?' said he. 'Let me see' and then the gaoler lifted her kerchief from her head and there were various spots on her face and one on her nose. Then said the Judge: 'In good faith, Agnes, when did he suck of thy blood last?' 'By my faith, good lord', said she, 'not for a fortnight.'

▼ **Source C** *This is woodcut from a pamphlet describing the trial of a woman accused of witchcraft. The accused person's hands were bound, a rope tied around the waist and they were then thrown into the water. If they sank they were innocent, if they floated, the Devil was holding them up and they were guilty.*

▼ **Source D** *Accusations of witchcraft that came to court between 1560 and 1700 in five counties*

County	No. of accusations 1560–1700	No. of executions 1560–1700
Sussex	33	1
Surrey	711	5
Hertfordshire	81	8
Kent	132	16
Essex	473 (50 of these were the work of Matthew Hopkins in 1645)	82
Total	1,430	112 (Altogether about 1,000 witches were executed in 200 years)

Source E *In 1587, a writer, George Gifford, describes how an accusation of witchcraft could arise.*

Some woman falls out with her neighbour. A suspicion arises. Within a few years she is in some jar with another neighbour. He becomes ill. The village gossips far and wide: Mother W is a witch; she has bewitched Mr B and two hogs have died unexpectedly.

Shortly afterwards someone else falls sick. The neighbours come to visit him. 'Well, neighbour,' says one, 'Did you ever anger Mother W?' 'Truly neighbour,' says he, 'my wife did ask her to keep her hens out of our garden.' Everybody now says that Mother W is a witch. It is beyond doubt, because someone saw a weasel run from her yard into his just as he became ill. The sick man dies, believing he is bewitched. Mother W is arrested and sent for trial.

A BACKGROUND INFORMATION

The background information is important: don't ignore it, even if you know the topic really well. You will probably find you can use it to support your answers. It gives you the theme, and the angle, of the enquiry.

B THE SOURCES

In your exam there will be six or seven sources. Here we have used five. Take some time with the sources: don't rush to the questions, however anxious you might be to find out what they want to know! Read the text sources carefully. Underline any key words. Don't just glance at the picture source: take time to look all around it, making sure you understand it properly. If you have some statistics, as here, do your best to work out what they mean – and what they don't mean. Don't forget to look at the provenance of every source: who wrote it, when, who they were, etc.

C TIMING

You don't have to worry about making any choices, just work your way through from Question 1 to Question 6. But you do need to think about timing. Look at the number of marks for each question: they vary quite a lot. You should try to answer a 6 mark question fairly briefly. If you do, you will find you have plenty of time to concentrate on the high-scoring last question.

Study the background information and the sources carefully. You are advised to spend at least ten minutes doing this. In answering the questions, you will need to use your knowledge of the topic to interpret and evaluate the sources.

Answer ALL the questions.

1 Study Source A.
   What can you learn from this source about attitudes to witchcraft at this time? [6]

2 Study Source B.
   Does this source prove that Agnes Waterhouse was a witch? Use the source and your own knowledge to explain your answer. [8]

3 Study Source D.
   Are you surprised by the information in this source? Use the source and your own knowledge to explain your answer. [8]

4 Study Sources A and D.
   How far do these two sources agree about how much attention the government gave to dealing with witchcraft? Use the sources and your own knowledge to explain your answer. [9]

5 Study Sources C and E.
   Is one of these sources more useful than the other as evidence about attitudes towards witchcraft? Use the sources and your own knowledge to explain your answer. [9]

6 Study **all** the sources.
   'Fear of witches was widespread in late 16th and 17th century England.' How far do the sources on this paper support that view? Use the sources and your own knowledge to explain your answer. Remember to identify the sources you use. [10]

D COMPREHENSION AND INFERENCE QUESTIONS

For this style of question you need to go beyond what is in front of you in the source and explain what else it tells you. See page 39.

E SOURCES IN THEIR CONTEXT

To answer questions like this, you have to put the source in context using your own knowledge. See page 75.

H EVALUATING AN INTERPRETATION

The final question asks you to use all the sources and your own knowledge to evaluate an interpretation, or point of view, put before you. It will always be partly true, and partly untrue, so find sources that support it and sources that contradict it, and then add some information from your own knowledge, before reaching a balanced judgement. See pages 118–119.

F COMPARING SOURCES

This question asks you to compare what two different sources say and to reach a judgement on how far they agree with each other. See pages 112–113.

G USEFULNESS QUESTIONS

This style of question asks you to evaluate how useful a source is for a particular historical enquiry. Make sure you use the provenance of the source to write about its strengths and weaknesses as evidence. See page 75.

Topic – Smuggling

Look below at the background information, the sources and the questions.

Background information

In the 18th century smuggling was very common. Goods were smuggled into the country along Britain's thousands of miles of unguarded coastline. This was because people wanted to avoid paying government taxes. These smuggled goods were cheaper and more attractive to people. Customs officers could do little to stop this trade and when they tried, juries often found the smugglers not guilty, as they didn't really consider smuggling to be a crime.

Source A

An account of smuggling by a visitor to a Cornish coastal village in 1799

In going down the hill we met several women whose appearance was so grotesque that I could not imagine how they had altered their natural appearance. We found out that they were villagers who were smuggling liquor which they were carrying in cows' bladders fastened under their petticoats. They were so heavily laden that it was with great difficulty that they waddled along.

Smuggling is carried on without the least worry of getting caught and without any interruptions from the customs officers. Smuggling seems to be a popular trade among the lower orders of people – and some hundreds gain their livelihood by it.

Source B

▲ A cartoon published in 1810. The woman is pretending to be pregnant and is taking the smuggled goods hidden under her dress into the local town where they will be sold.

Source C

A newspaper report (from 1748) about the trial of members of the Hawkhurst gang. The Hawkhurst gang were a well-known gang of smugglers in Dorset and other parts of southern England. Galley had been escorting Chater, who had identified one of the gang, to the trial.

The smugglers began with the customs officer Galley, cut off his nose and the private parts, broke every bone in his body and after several hours of torture killed him. Chater, an informer, they carried to a dry well, hung him from a cross beam leaving him to die with hunger and pain; but when they came, several days after, and heard him groan, they cut the rope, let him drop to the bottom, and threw in logs and stones to cover him. The person who gave this information in court was in disguise to prevent him from suffering the same fate.

1 Study Sources A and B. Are you surprised by the actions of the women in these two sources? Use the sources and your own knowledge to explain your answer. [8]

2 How useful is Source C in finding out about smuggling in the 1700s? [8]

Placing a source in its historical context

To answer Question 1 effectively you need to combine details from the sources with your own knowledge of the period. It is important that you consider the **historical context**. At first glance it may seem incredible to think that people thought it was acceptable to break the law and smuggle goods. But you **need to consider people's attitudes to this crime in the 18th century**. As you should have realised by now, people's attitudes are really important in the history of crime and punishment. One analogy to use is people's attitudes today to file sharing on the internet. Is this type of crime taken seriously by the millions who do it? Do they actually think that they are breaking the law?

Evaluating sources

Question 2 asks you to evaluate how useful Source C is for finding out about smuggling in the 1700s. There is more to this question than meets the eye. That is why it is worth 8 marks. You need to consider the **strengths and limitations** of Source C.

Remember the question is asking you how **useful** the source is, not how **useless**. There won't be any sources that are completely useless. Do not get bogged down telling the examiner what is wrong with the source. Begin and end your answer positively.

Use the grid below to develop an effective answer.

	Strengths	Limitations
Step 1: Consider content • What do we learn? How is this useful? • What do we not learn? What is missed out? What else would you want to know?	Source C is useful because … … it helps us understand how ruthless smuggling gangs actually were. We can learn that they were prepared to use physical violence and even murder to protect and save members of their gang. This could suggest they were feared by normal people because they were prepared to go to such extreme measures.	However, Source C … … only tells us about how this gang protected each other. The source doesn't tell us how goods were smuggled, or what types of goods were smuggled, or how ordinary people viewed smugglers.
Step 2: Consider the provenance of the source • What is the **nature** of the source? What **type of source** is it? • What are the **origins** of the source? **Who** wrote or produced the source? **When** was it produced? • What was the **purpose** of the source? **Why** was it produced? • **How typical** is the source of the period and other sources? Do other sources back it up? How do the above affect its usefulness?	Source C is a newspaper report from 1748. Newspapers were written to report on local events. This would suggest that the source is telling the truth about the Hawkhurst gang and reporting on it.	However, we need to be careful about totally accepting this report as an impression of smugglers. The report may have highlighted the gruesome nature of the attacks on Galley and Chater to grab the reader's attention and sell copies of the newspaper. Also it only describes the actions of one violent gang involved in smuggling in one year: 1748. To check to see if all smugglers were violent we need to look at other sources. For example … we would also need to consider smuggling before and after 1748.
Step 3: Reach an overall judgement Always end with a conclusion in which you reach your judgement. • How useful is the source (very, quite)? • What is your key reason for reaching this judgement?		Overall the source is … extremely / very / quite / not very useful for a historian studying …

Early Modern Period summary: why was the Bloody Code introduced?

You now know a lot about crimes in this period. But we haven't fully addressed the really big issue of punishments. As you found out on page 58, the number of crimes carrying the death penalty increased dramatically. Why did so many crimes become punishable by death between 1690 and 1815? Why was the Bloody Code introduced?

Activity

Why was the Bloody Code introduced? Stage 1

If you were asked to research the Bloody Code for homework where would you look first? An internet encyclopaedia site? But how do you know that the information you gleaned from the internet is true? After all, anyone can write an entry or amend what is said on some of these sites. Look at this entry below. It seems very knowledgeable. But in reality it isn't. It's hopeless. There are lots of mistakes! Your task is to use the sources to spot the mistakes and improve the entry.

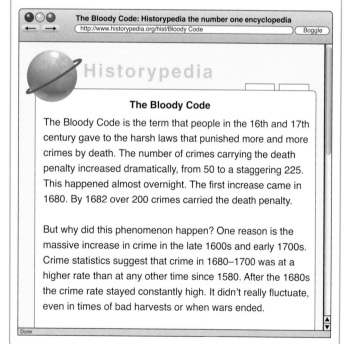

The Bloody Code: Historypedia the number one encyclopedia

http://www.historypedia.org/hist/Bloody Code   Boggle

Historypedia

The Bloody Code

The Bloody Code is the term that people in the 16th and 17th century gave to the harsh laws that punished more and more crimes by death. The number of crimes carrying the death penalty increased dramatically, from 50 to a staggering 225. This happened almost overnight. The first increase came in 1680. By 1682 over 200 crimes carried the death penalty.

But why did this phenomenon happen? One reason is the massive increase in crime in the late 1600s and early 1700s. Crime statistics suggest that crime in 1680–1700 was at a higher rate than at any other time since 1580. After the 1680s the crime rate stayed constantly high. It didn't really fluctuate, even in times of bad harvests or when wars ended.

Done

▲ A mass public execution in London, painted by a French revolutionary artist, Theodore Gericault

Source 2

A gradual increase in capital punishments

Through the 1600s the number of crimes carrying the death penalty rose. In 1723 the Waltham Black Act added 50 new capital crimes. The number gradually increased. By 1765, it had risen to 160.

People in the 16th and 17th centuries didn't use the term, 'Bloody Code'. This was the name critics of harsh punishments gave to it later on.

Source 3

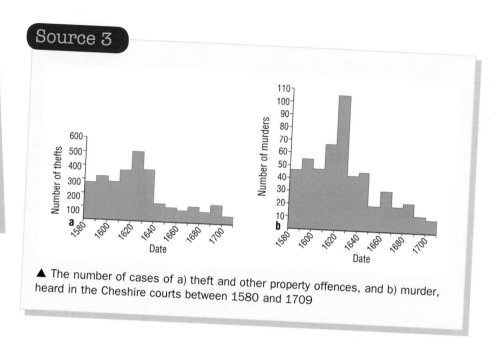

▲ The number of cases of a) theft and other property offences, and b) murder, heard in the Cheshire courts between 1580 and 1709

Source 4

Serious crime in Devon

In Devon, courts heard about 250 serious cases a year in the early 1600s, but only 38 by 1700. The rate of murder fell from eight per cent per 100,000 people to just one per cent per 100,000 people in 1700.

Source 5

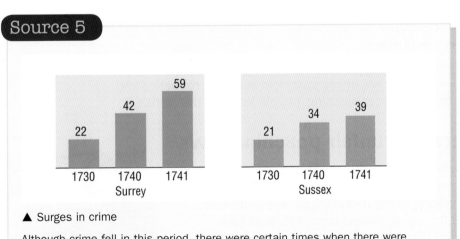

▲ Surges in crime

Although crime fell in this period, there were certain times when there were surges in crime. The two graphs above show average theft rates in Surrey and Sussex. Food prices had been low in the 1730s. But two bad harvests were followed by a cold winter in 1739–1740. The River Thames froze and coal from Newcastle didn't arrive. Those who struggled in good years found themselves in desperate conditions.

Activity

Why was the Bloody Code introduced? Stage 2

Below is the next paragraph of the hopeless internet encyclopaedia site for the Bloody Code. Again it is littered with mistakes. You need to use the knowledge that you now have about crimes in this period (look back to pages 64–71 if you are unsure) to correct this part of the entry.

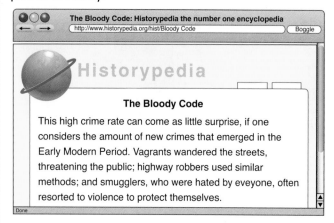

The Bloody Code: Historypedia the number one encyclopedia

http://www.historypedia.org/hist/Bloody Code   Boggle

Historypedia

The Bloody Code

This high crime rate can come as little surprise, if one considers the amount of new crimes that emerged in the Early Modern Period. Vagrants wandered the streets, threatening the public; highway robbers used similar methods; and smugglers, who were hated by eveyone, often resorted to violence to protect themselves.

Done

On the right are the final two paragraphs on the Bloody Code. Again you need to correct the mistakes. Use the information below and on the opposite page to help you.

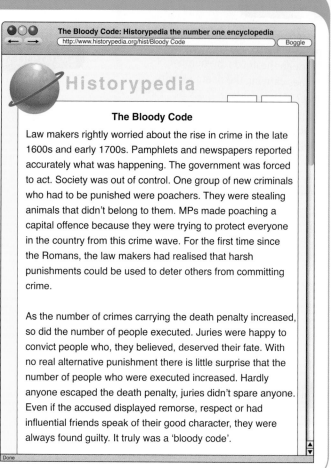

The Bloody Code: Historypedia the number one encyclopedia

http://www.historypedia.org/hist/Bloody Code   Boggle

Historypedia

The Bloody Code

Law makers rightly worried about the rise in crime in the late 1600s and early 1700s. Pamphlets and newspapers reported accurately what was happening. The government was forced to act. Society was out of control. One group of new criminals who had to be punished were poachers. They were stealing animals that didn't belong to them. MPs made poaching a capital offence because they were trying to protect everyone in the country from this crime wave. For the first time since the Romans, the law makers had realised that harsh punishments could be used to deter others from committing crime.

As the number of crimes carrying the death penalty increased, so did the number of people executed. Juries were happy to convict people who, they believed, deserved their fate. With no real alternative punishment there is little surprise that the number of people who were executed increased. Hardly anyone escaped the death penalty, juries didn't spare anyone. Even if the accused displayed remorse, respect or had influential friends speak of their good character, they were always found guilty. It truly was a 'bloody code'.

Done

The influence of printing

Law makers were worried about crime even though we now know that it was falling. It is human nature to think that crime is a serious problem. There was plenty of evidence at the time to alarm the law makers and the public about the levels of crime.

There were many reports in broadsheets about vagabonds and highwaymen. These early newspapers gave lurid details of robberies and murders. Although they were misleading, people believed the stories.

Landowners and unfair poaching laws

The MPs who passed the laws that made up the Bloody Code were rich landowners. After 1688, these rich landowners had the power to pass laws. Some historians believe that these landowners used the law to protect their own land and privileges. They cite laws against poachers as evidence.

Poaching, like smuggling, was not considered a crime by most ordinary people. In fact, the laws against poaching were some of the most unpopular in the 1700s. Only landowners whose land was worth £100 a year could hunt and they could hunt **anywhere**. Other landowners with land worth less than £100 **could not even hunt on their own land**. Roughly 97 per cent of the population did not own any land at all. In 1723, the Black Act said that hunting deer, hare or rabbits was punishable by death. Anyone found armed, disguised or with a blackened face in any hunting area was assumed to be poaching and could be executed.

Critics of these laws believed they were designed simply to protect the interests of the landowners in Parliament. Many saw poaching as an ancient custom that was a right long before the landowners enclosed the land in the 1700s.

The number of executions fell after 1688

Source 6

	1600–1610	1700–1710
London	150	20
Devon	25	3

▲ A comparison of executions (averages per year) in London and Devon.

smarter revision tips

You could use a **memory map** to pull together all you know about crime and punishment in the Early Modern Period. See pages 20–21 to remind you of how to construct your own memory map. The main branches could be: Crime, Policing, Punishment and Trials.

You could also make **revision cards** to help you revise an important topic like the Bloody Code. See pages 32–33 to remind yourself how to make revision cards.

A **timeline** would help you understand *when* things happened, and how all the events *fit together*. See page 11 for how to make and use a timeline.

Juries were unwilling to find people guilty of some crimes because they thought that the punishment did not fit the crime. Around 30 per cent of accused people were acquitted. Even more were found guilty of stealing goods of a lower value. Many others were let off because witnesses spoke about their good character and law-abiding nature. A famous actor, Charles Macklin, got away with murdering another actor after an argument. This was because he had plenty of important witnesses who spoke up for him. He was found guilty of manslaughter and branded on the hand.

Anyone showing remorse or respect for the court was likely to escape hanging. Executions fell because of the development of other punishments. Transportation to the American colonies was seen as an alternative to the death penalty. During the wars against France, from 1680 to 1714, criminals were offered the chance to serve in the army or the navy.

Activity

Look back to page 58. You were asked to predict what factors would have helped bring about the Bloody Code.

Can you identify and explain the factors that you now think helped to bring about this Bloody Code?

In the first four chapters of this book you have studied over 2,500 years of crime and punishment. In many ways little had changed since the time of the Roman Empire. Rulers and governments had nearly all chosen the same solution to the problem of crime – savage and bloody punishments that were meant to frighten people and deter them from committing a crime.

Now get ready for some major changes – a revolution in fact!

Activities

1. Work in pairs. You have five minutes. What evidence can you find in this picture of:
   a. different crimes
   b. different punishments
   c. different forms of policing/crime prevention
   d. different trials.
2. You now have three minutes. How many *similarities* can you find between crime, punishment, trials and policing in the Industrial Period and the Early Modern Period?
3. Now you have two minutes. What *differences* can you find between crime, punishment, trials and policing in the Industrial Period and the Early Modern Period?
4. What seem to be the big changes in crimes and punishments in this period?

Criminal moment in time 4: London 1845

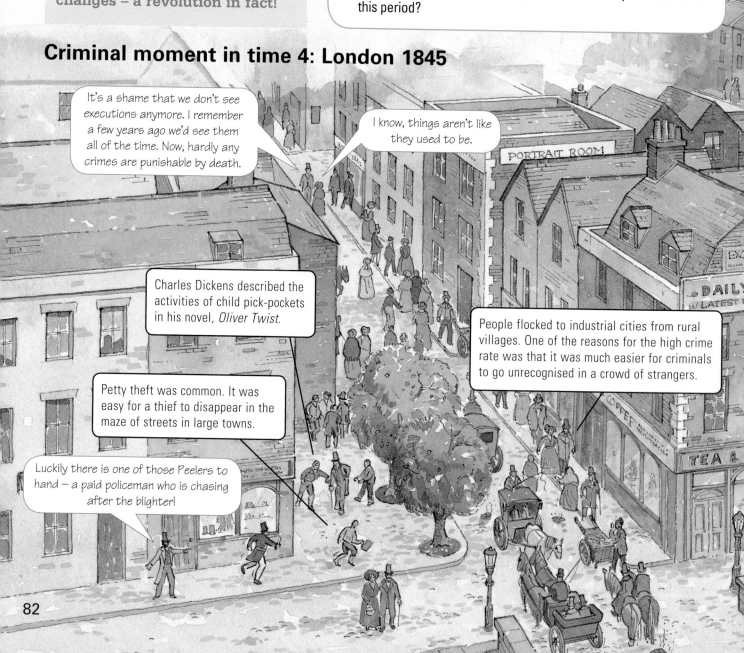

It's a shame that we don't see executions anymore. I remember a few years ago we'd see them all of the time. Now, hardly any crimes are punishable by death.

I know, things aren't like they used to be.

Charles Dickens described the activities of child pick-pockets in his novel, *Oliver Twist*.

People flocked to industrial cities from rural villages. One of the reasons for the high crime rate was that it was much easier for criminals to go unrecognised in a crowd of strangers.

Petty theft was common. It was easy for a thief to disappear in the maze of streets in large towns.

Luckily there is one of those Peelers to hand – a paid policeman who is chasing after the blighter!

Information

The Industrial Revolution

As you have already seen several times in this book, the story of crime reflects the story of what else was happening in Britain at the time. For example, in Section 4 you saw how changes in religious beliefs led to the creation of a new crime: vagrancy – as well as a rise in the number of witchcraft trials. In the years after 1750, Britain became the first country in the world to industrialise. It changed the lives of everyone in the country. It was a real revolution.

Prisons became an important form of punishment. Prisoners either worked in silence, or were kept separate from each other. They were given religious instruction. The authorities hoped that this would help them **reform**.

Fast transport made it easy for criminals to get away.

Royal judges visited counties four times a year. They were experts in the law. They judged serious crimes. At the royal courts, a jury was still used.

The judge listened to the evidence and decided that I should pay a fine of 10 shillings for stealing the piece of bread.

How are we going to pay? We can't afford to eat.

Large numbers of convicts were transported to Australia.

5.1 The Big Story – why was there a revolution in punishment and policing in the years 1750–1900?

A CALENDAR of the PRISONERS that are to
be tried at the Assizes, 1786.
FELONS in DURHAM GAOL

JANE SCOTT, committed by Robert Ilderton, Esq; charged upon Oath of Edward Thompson, with having stolen one stuff quilted Petticoat, one Muslin Apron, two linen Shifts; with several other Articles of wearing Apparel, of the Value of 20s. the Property of the said Edward Thompson.

ROBERT BELL, committed by the Honourable Thomas Lyon, charged with having on the 14th of May, 1786, feloniously stolen out of the Stable of Mr Robert Wade, at Fatfield, about One Bushel of Oats.

JOHN HALL, committed by Anthony Hall, Esq; charged with having feloniously stolen, several Articles of wearing Apparel, one Guinea in Gold, and two Half Crown Pieces, in Silver, the Property of George Scott.

JOHN DIDSBURY, committed by the Rev. Robert Thorp, charged with having feloniously stolen in the Dwelling house of George Holmes, sundry Articles of wearing Apparel, the Property of the said George Holmes.

WILLIAM STONEHOUSE, committed by the Rev. Henry Ellison, charged with having feloniously stolen, one Shirt and one Shift, the Value of ten Pence, the Property of Robert Maddison.

THOMAS HAY, committed by William Ettrick, Esq; charged with stealing out of the Stable of Thomas White, of Sunderland, on the 10th of January, 1786, one bay Mare, the Property of the said Thomas White.

EDWARD PERKIN, committed by William Ettrick, Esq; charged with having feloniously and burglariously breaking and entering the Dwelling House of John Greenfield, of Sunderland, Innkeeper, and stealing therein two Silk Handkerchiefs and a Piece of Leathern Pouch, of the Value of 5s.

JOHN REED, committed by the Rev. Cooper Abbs, charged with having broken the Dwelling-house of William Trail, of Monkwearmouth, and stealing therein, one Silver Watch of Value of Forty Shillings, two Guineas in Gold, on Crown Piece, four Half Crown Pieces, and Six Shillings in Silver, with other Articles.

JOHN SUTCLIFFE, committed by Henry Mills, Esq; charged upon the Oaths of John Marshall and Charles Wright with having stolen a Silver Pint, the Property of the said John Marshall.

▲ A 'calendar' (list) of prisoners tried at Durham Assize court in 1786. We have removed the punishments.

Activities

1 On your copy of Table 1 below, fill out columns 2 and 3. In column 3 try to predict which of the following punishments you think each criminal in Source 1 received:
   - whipped
   - hanged
   - fined
   - transported to Australia.

2 Check the actual punishments on page 138, then fill in columns 4 and 5 to see if your predictions were right. How many predictions did you get right?

3 Does anything about the records surprise you?

4 What does this court record tell you about crime, punishment and policing in the late 1700s? You will need to infer (read between the lines). For example, the number of 'no bill' entries suggests there was no effective police force. With no police force, crime was probably much higher than the records show.

5 Now, on your own, read between the lines and write a short paragraph: 'My findings about crime and punishment in 1786'. Think about:
   - what punishments were used
   - what punishments you expected to see but weren't used
   - what crimes the judges took seriously
   - what this suggests about the law makers
   - what types of crime were common. What does this suggest?
   - whether the punishments were random or consistent. What does this tell you?

Table 1: 1786

Name	Crime committed	My punishment prediction	Actual punishment	Correct?
Jane Scott				
Robert Bell				
John Hall				
John Didsbury				
William Stonehouse				
Thomas Hay				
Edward Perkin				
John Reed				
John Sutcliffe				

Source 2

DURHAM.

James Boyd, 30, for stealing several articles of wearing apparel. *death recorded.*

Nicholas Urwin, 28, and Thomas Smith, 29, severally charged with having carnally known Mary Dodds, against her will. *guilty, DEATH.*

Robert Gilbert, 26, for stealing a silver watch, two sovereigns, and other articles. *death recd.*

Joseph Develin, 24, for cutting and wounding Jacob Mills. *no bill.*

Richard Fairlamb, 20, for killing and slaying Ed. Mackey. *fined 1s. and discharged.*

William Brown, 19, *1 month*, Henderson Brown, 32, *6 months*, Edward Brown, 30, *2 ms.* and James Coxon, 28, severally charged with having attempted to drown Mark Allen.

Thomas Corner, 21, for setting fire to a hay stack. *not guilty.*

William Smith, alias Noblet, 52, for stealing a mare. *transported for life.*

John Scott, 17, for killing and slaying Luke Thompson. *acquitted.*

Robert Rawling, 32, with having received a mare, well knowing the same to have been stolen. *transported for life.*

Francis Snaith, 40, for stealing a cow. *aqtd.*

William Bullerwell, 36, for stealing a two-gallon cask of rum. *3 months hard labour.*

Thomas Hollingsworth, 20, for entering a building, the property of the Stocton and Darlington Railway Company. *trans. for life.*

Henry Dove, 19, for stealing a quantity of old iron. *transported 7 years.*

Mary Rawling, 37, for stealing a cart wheel. *no bill.*

Robert Haswell, 18, for stealing a pair of boots. *transported 7 years.*

Isaac Edrehi, 25, for stealing a five pound promissory note. *acquitted.*

Thomas Cockerill, 22, for stealing one five pound note and two sovereigns. *12 months.*

◀ Sentences passed at Durham Assizes, 1836

Now let's move forward 50 years and go to the Durham Assizes records again, this time in 1836. Source 2 is less detailed than Source 1 but it shows the sentences handed down by the judges.

(Note: 'No bill' – means there wasn't enough evidence to prosecute.)

Activities

6 Use a copy of Table 2 to record the punishments given.

7 a Have punishments changed?

   b Has anything else changed?

8 Use these records and read between the lines to record what you think the big changes are to:
   • crime
   • punishments
   • policing.

Table 2: 1836

Name	Crime committed	Actual punishment
James Boyd		
Nicholas Urwin and Thomas Smith		
Robert Gilbert		
Richard Fairlamb		
William Brown, Henderson Brown and James Coxon		
William Smith		
Robert Rawling		
William Bullerwell		
Thomas Hollingsworth		
Robert Haswell		
Thomas Cockerill		

5.2 How did crime change in industrial Britain – and why?

Now that you know about the changes in overview you are going to examine each area of change one by one. This first enquiry is about *crime*. What changed and why?

Source 1

▲ The Artful Dodger introduces Oliver Twist to Fagin, Bill Sikes and Nancy. This is a drawing to accompany Charles Dickens' novel *Oliver Twist*, published in 1839. Oliver is an innocent orphan who finds himself in London. The Artful Dodger is the leader of a gang of child criminals; Fagin deals in stolen property; Bill Sikes is a violent criminal; and Nancy, a prostitute, is his partner.

Source 2

In *Oliver Twist*, Dickens describes Bill Sikes as below. ('Fetters' are heavy chains put round a criminal's ankles to stop him running away.)

A stoutly-built fellow of about five-and-thirty, in a black velveteen coat, very soiled drab breeches, lace-up half boots, and grey cotton stockings which inclosed a bulky pair of legs, with large swelling calves, — the kind of legs, which always look in an incomplete state without a set of fetters to garnish them. He had a brown hat on his head, and a dirty handkerchief round his neck: with the long frayed ends of which he smeared the beer from his face as he spoke. He had a broad heavy countenance with a beard of three weeks' growth, and two scowling eyes, one of which displayed various symptoms of having been recently damaged by a blow.

Charles Dickens' novel *Oliver Twist* describes a London that is a thieves' paradise. Young pick-pockets like the Artful Dodger roamed the streets, while bigger, violent thieves like Bill Sikes were supported by a criminal network similar to Fagin's. Dickens' middle-class readers were horrified – and couldn't get enough of it! *Oliver Twist* was a huge success.

But was it true? Historians can use evidence from contemporary novels, but also put other sources alongside them. Source 3 shows the crime statistics for this period.

Source 3

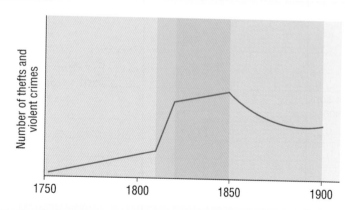

▲ A graph showing trends in crime, 1750–1900

Activities

Study Source 3.

1 What happened to the levels of crime in the four periods: 1750–1810, 1810–1820, 1820–1850, 1850–1900?

2 What three questions would you want to ask about the picture Source 3 gives of changes in crime in Britain during this period?

3 Now use the information in the boxes opposite to suggest answers to your three questions.

What made London a thieves' paradise?

Population
In 1750 there were 9.5 million people in England and Wales. By 1850 there were 27 million. London was the biggest city in Europe. Its population quadrupled: 1760 – 750,000; 1860 – 3,000,000.

Harvests
Food prices had always depended on the quality of the harvest. If the harvest was bad then the poor were in danger of starvation.

Hunger can turn many people to crime.

Towns and cities
People flocked to the growing towns in the hope of finding work. They often found themselves living in overcrowded and unhealthy conditions.

Family life was disrupted. People lost the controls and support of family and village. Who cared if you turned to crime?

Built-up area

River Thames

Extent of London, c.1850

Communications
There were spectacular improvements in transport, with docks and canals, and by 1850 there were 10,000 miles (16,000km) of railway in Britain.

There were more opportunities for crime, too, with ships, warehouses, barges, wagons and trains to be burgled – and provide a fast getaway!

Governments
For centuries British people resisted any attempt by the government to interfere in their lives. This was just beginning to change. Income tax was introduced for the first time in the 1790s to help pay for the war against France. Governments began to think about reforms, which they hoped would improve the country – by dealing with crime.

But until 1829 London had no police force. Did this help to make it a thieves' paradise?

Work
In 1750 most people worked by farming the land. By 1850 most people worked in factories, mines or offices. Hours were long and working conditions were harsh. Jobs were uncertain, with workers laid off at a moment's notice with nothing to live on. Poverty was always close by.

Did crime offer an easier alternative to honest work when times were hard?

The later 19th century

But what about the fourth section of the crime statistics graph, Source 3? By 1900:

- working hours were a bit shorter and there had been some improvement in working conditions
- living conditions were beginning to improve
- the first cars had appeared; telegrams whizzed along the wires carrying news faster than ever before
- after 1885 most men were able to vote
- bad harvests were not so vital. Food could be imported cheaply and quickly from abroad thanks to the changes in transport
- only 5 per cent of the population could not read or write.

Activities

4 Use the information on this page to suggest reasons for the trends in crime in the graph, Source 3.

5 How do you think these changes in crime would affect:
- punishments
- policing?

6 Make a note of what you predict, and see if you were right as you go through the rest of this section.

5.3 How did punishment change in industrial Britain – and why?

The Industrial Revolution changed Britain in lots of ways, including – as we have seen – the amount of crime. So get ready for some big changes to punishment too. In particular, by 1850 the Bloody Code had been swept away. The only crimes punishable by death were murder and treason. The number of executions had fallen to an average of eleven per year. Not only that, public executions ended in 1868. Prison became the most common punishment. And prisons were totally reformed from chaotic, squalid death-traps to efficient and tightly controlled institutions.

In this enquiry you will find out more about these changes.

Big changes in history usually have many causes. In the introduction to this book, pages 4–5, you were introduced to the **nine key factors** affecting crime. You can see them on the right.

Prison reformers

Later in this section we will be asking how the nine key factors played their part in the big reforms of this period. But reform often starts with just a few people, so we are going to start by looking at the lives of three key individuals: Elizabeth Fry, John Howard and Samuel Romilly. You can see our first reformer simply by looking at a £5 note.

Elizabeth Fry, 1780–1845

In 1800, most prisons were terrible places: unsuitable buildings; unhealthy environments; with prisoners of all types locked in together. But women's prisons were worse. Women prisoners had not only broken the law, they had also broken society's expectations that a woman should be an angel, a home-builder, gentle and good. Yet there were four times more women in prison in Elizabeth Fry's day, in proportion to the population, than there are today.

Elizabeth Fry came from a well-off Quaker family of bankers. Quakers do not have paid ministers and anyone can speak at a Meeting for Worship – men or women – so Quaker women were perhaps more liberated than many women at the time. Quakers also believe that there is something of God in everyone, and that has drawn many of them to work in prisons. It was what led Elizabeth Fry to visit the women's section of Newgate prison, London, in December 1813.

Fry was horrified at what she found: 300 women were crammed into three rooms – shouting, fighting, crying – many with babies and small children.

Activity

Whose picture should be on the £5 note?

Does Elizabeth Fry alone deserve this accolade? Are Howard and Romilly neglected heroes?

Over the next four pages you can research each of these three individuals and decide who most deserves to be on the £5 note. You will then support your decision with evidence from their lives.

Source 1

▲ Elizabeth Fry's portrait on a £5 note

Source 2

Elizabeth Fry's letter to three of her children: John (9), William (7) and her daughter Richenda (5), written on 13 February 1813

I have lately been twice to Newgate to see after the poor prisoners who had poor little infants without clothing, or with very little and I think if you saw how small a piece of bread they are each allowed a day you would be very sorry.

I hope, if you should live to grow up, you will endeavour to be very useful and not spend all your time in pleasing yourself.

Their jailers were male and often exploited the fact that the prisoners were dependent on them for food, bedding, clothes, medicine and any kind of help (Source 2). Fry never forgot the sight of two women ripping the clothes off a dead baby to put on a living one. She returned the next day with some clean straw bedding and baby clothes.

Gradually, after many visits, Fry won the trust of the women. She led prayers with them and started a school for their children (Source 3). She wanted them to be able to live useful lives when they were freed, not fall back on theft and prostitution because they had no other means of surviving. So she taught them 'useful work' like sewing and knitting, and sold their products for them.

Impact

Fry became famous in her own lifetime (Source 4). She met Queen Victoria and travelled to many countries to encourage them to reform their prisons. She had a big influence on the 1825 Gaols Act. This ensured that women's prisons should be separate from men's, with female staff. The prisoners should be supplied with clothing, food and bedding. The Act also set up the system of prison visitors to ensure that prisoners were decently treated.

However, as the years went on, attitudes changed. Prisons were to be places where inmates were punished, not reformed. Later reformers sneered at her 'good works' (Sources 5 and 6). When her husband's bank went bust Fry was accused of neglecting him and their eleven children. There was no place for her 'useful work' in the prisons of 'Hard labour, Hard fare, Hard board' of late 19th century prisons (see page 99).

Source 3

Elizabeth Fry's journal entry, 24 February 1817

I have lately been occupied in forming a school in Newgate for the children of the poor prisoners as well as the young criminals, which has brought much peace and satisfaction with it; but my mind has also been deeply affected in attending a poor woman who was executed this morning. I visited her twice; this has been a time of deep humiliation to me, this witnessing the effect of the consequences of sin. The poor creature murdered her baby; and how inexpressibly awful now to have her life taken away.

Source 4

John Randolph, American Envoy to England (February 1819)

I have seen Elizabeth Fry in Newgate and I have witnessed there miraculous effects of true Christianity upon the most depraved of human beings.

Source 5

In the 1840s Edwin Chadwick comments on the work of Elizabeth Fry and John Howard

Because of the Howards and Frys, the prisons have been so reformed by narrow sentiment and blind zeal as to actually attract vagrants and others who prefer their comfort to working.

Source 6

Comments from a critic of Elizabeth Fry in the 1840s

Elizabeth Fry was committed to reforming the prisoners by work, rather than punishing them by hard labour.

John Howard, 1726–1790

When John Howard's father, a wealthy London shopkeeper, died, John bought a country estate in Bedfordshire. In 1773, he was appointed sheriff of the county. For most upper-class landowners who were made sheriff it was just a title and they usually appointed an under-sheriff to do the work. John Howard, however, took the job seriously. One of his duties was to inspect the prisons in Bedfordshire.

Howard was shocked by what he saw and began to visit other prisons all over the country. What he found was published in a report in 1777: *The State of Prisons in England and Wales* (see Sources 1, 2 and 3). It contained detailed plans and descriptions of the chaotic state of British prisons in the late 18th century.

Howard believed that being in prison itself was the punishment; it did not have to be a punishing experience. He particularly criticised the system by which people who were too poor to pay the jailer's fee had to stay in prison even though they had served their sentence. His proposals for improvement included healthy buildings, separation of prisoners, a decent diet, better warders and a system of inspection.

Impact

The report alerted Britain to the scandalous state of its prisons. However, real reform only began some time after Howard's death, in the 1820s and 1830s. When prisons did begin to change, his practical proposals for healthy, separate cells were taken up, but his emphasis on reforming prisoners, rather than punishing them, brought him the same criticism as Elizabeth Fry (see pages 88–89).

However, the need to make prisons decent places, from which people could emerge better than when they went in, continues to this day and his name lives on in the Howard League for Penal Reform (see www.howardleague.org).

Source 1

Some details from John Howard's report, *The State of Prisons in England and Wales*, 1777

- Many prisoners who were found not guilty could not get out of prison because they could not afford the discharge fee set by the jailer.

- Debtors' prisons had few warders and the prisoners could not be chained or forced to work. In the Marshalsea prison in London butchers and other tradesmen came into the prison to sell food or play skittles with the prisoners in the prison drinking room. A chandler had four rooms in the prison. He used one as his workroom and shop, two for his family and sub-let the last room to other prisoners.

- In prisons where debtors were mixed with serious criminals the warders let the criminals have the same privileges as the debtors. There were not enough warders to keep them separate.

- Prisoners already in a cell forced new prisoners to pay a fee to them known as 'garnish'. Warders did little to stop this.

- In some gaols you see boys of 12 and 13 eagerly listening to the stories told by experienced criminals, of their adventures, successes and escapes.

Source 2

Extracts from John Howard's report on Gloucester gaol, 1777

Gaoler – William Williams. Salary – None
Chaplain – Mr Evans. Salary – £40
Surgeon – None
1 June 1777 Total prisoners – 16 debtors, 24 criminals
There is only one small day room 12 feet by 11 for men and women criminals. The ward for debtors is 19 feet by 11, has no window so part of the plaster wall is broken down for light and air. The night room for male criminals is close and dark and the floor so ruinous that it cannot be washed. The whole prison is much out of repair.

Many prisoners died here in 1773. Eight died about Christmas of smallpox. There is no proper separation of the women. Five or six children have lately been born in the gaol.

Source 3

Extracts from John Howard's report on Newgate gaol (London), 1777

The sallow faces declare, without words, that they are very miserable; many who went in healthy are, in a few months, changed to emaciated dejected objects. Some are dying on the floors, in loathsome cells, of fevers and smallpox.

Samuel Romilly, 1757–1818

Samuel Romilly came from a French Huguenot family who had fled to England in 1685. He kept up links with France and was a supporter of the early years of the French Revolution. He became a successful lawyer, went into politics, and was often a radical critic of the government.

Romilly was influenced by the Italian writer Beccaria (Source 4) and criticised the Bloody Code as cruel and illogical. Cruel, because it put people to death for minor offences; illogical because few of those condemned were actually hanged, and the sentence often relied on the whim of the judge.

Impact

Romilly succeeded in removing the death penalty for several offences, including pick-pocketing (in 1808)

and sailors or soldiers found begging. He tried but failed to have the death penalty removed from petty theft and burglary. But times were changing in Romilly's lifetime, with far fewer executions being carried out and a change of attitude towards crime and punishment (Source 5).

After Romilly died, the death penalty was gradually removed from all offences except murder and treason.

Source 4

In 1767 Cesare Beccaria's book *On Crimes and Punishments* was published in English. This is an extract from his book.

The punishments do not stop crime. Instead of making a terrifying example of a few criminals we should punish all criminals and punish them fairly. We need punishments that fit the crime. Instead of relying on the death penalty, criminals should be imprisoned and do hard labour that is visible to the public.

Activity

Review

So whose face most deserves to be on the £5 note: Elizabeth Fry, John Howard or Samuel Romilly?

Make your choice and write a letter to the Royal Mint (who design and print the £5 note), **either**:

- congratulating them on their choice of Elizabeth Fry and explaining why you agree with them, **or**
- telling the Royal Mint which other reformer ought to be commemorated in this way, and why.

Source 5

Average numbers of people sentenced to death and executions, 1805–1854

	Death sentences per year	Executions per year	% of those executed who were condemned for murder
1805–1814	443	66	20
1815–1824	1073	89	18
1825–1834	1218	53	23
1835–1844	199	13	77
1845–1854	57	9	100

Transportation: success or failure?

In the early 1800s the Bloody Code was gradually discarded. Execution was used only for murder and even then often reluctantly. The courts increasingly preferred the less severe punishment of transportation. But was it a good alternative?

Activity

The year is 1850. Britain has been using transportation for over 60 years, with more than 2,500 convicts being transported each year – in 1833, the peak year, 6,779 were transported. But doubts are being raised about the transportation policy:

- people in Australia object. The colony is becoming more successful. More and more people are migrating there willingly to set up a new life. Australia would prefer to receive more free migrants, not more criminals

- at home in Britain, questions are also being asked. Is transportation successful? It is quite expensive to send ships on four-month journeys round the world – is it doing what it is supposed to do?

You are a civil servant who has been asked to look into the problem and write a report for the Minister.

Step 1: Find out about the history of transportation

Use the text and sources on pages 92–95 to find out more about transportation.

Use the questions here to guide your enquiry:

> When did transportation start?
> Why was it introduced?
> … and why Australia?
> Who was transported?
> What happened to the convicts?

When did transportation start?

The British government had been getting rid of people they didn't want, such as rebels and criminals, since the 1660s – to America. Then, in the 1780s, Britain faced a crisis. The American colonies had won their independence so transportation to what was now the USA stopped suddenly. For a while convicts were put in prisons and hulks (ships used as prisons – see page 94) but they soon became overcrowded. Another colony was desperately needed to accommodate Britain's criminals.

Several colonies, including the West Indian islands, were considered. The last was the scarcely known colony of Australia, which had only been discovered in 1770 by James Cook. There was no possibility of sending anyone to find out whether Australia would be a good convict settlement – the round trip would take eighteen months! So the first settlers and convicts were sent out without any real idea of what they were going to encounter.

The first fleet set sail for Australia in May 1787. Eleven ships left Portsmouth, carrying 1,020 people, of whom 736 were convicts (sentenced to transportation for seven years, fourteen years, or for life). The youngest was nine-year-old John Hudson, the oldest 82-year-old Dorothy Handland. Most had committed minor offences, like the West Indian man Thomas Chaddick who had stolen twelve cucumber plants.

Eight months later they landed in Australia. Forty-eight had died on the voyage, a surprisingly low number, given that transportation to Australia was new and poorly planned. Few of the convicts had any useful skills. There were just two brick-makers, two bricklayers, six carpenters and a stonemason – and shelter was required for over 1,000 people! It was a small miracle that they survived to welcome the next fleet, which didn't arrive for another two years!

Why was transportation introduced … and why Australia?

To provide an alternative to hanging. While the Bloody Code was the law, many people felt that hanging was too extreme a punishment for minor crimes. Juries would not convict people and judges would find excuses not to hang people. There were few prisons and building new ones would be very expensive. Transportation was the 'middle' punishment between the extremes of execution and the milder whipping or pillory, which were being used much less by this time.

1

To deter criminals. Australia was unknown and the government hoped that the idea of being sent to the edge of the world would terrify people and so stop them breaking the law.

2

To get rid of criminals. Transportation of criminals would reduce crime in Britain by reducing the number in the criminal class.

3

To reform criminals. Criminals would be forced to work and learn skills that would be useful when they were freed. (This was the least important reason behind transportation – but it worked. Transported criminals were more likely to lead law-abiding lives after release than criminals who had been sent to prison in Britain.)

4

To help the settlement and development of Australia as part of the British Empire. Transportation would help Britain to claim Australia for her empire. This would stop France or other rivals gaining whatever resources Australia had.

5

Who was transported?

A typical convict arriving in Australia was a young man of 26 who had been convicted several times for theft, usually of food, clothing or goods of a small value. He had grown up in a town but had no skills or regular job. Eighty per cent of the convicts sent to Australia were thieves and most had committed more than one offence. Only three per cent had been convicted of violent crimes.

Far more men than women were sent to Australia. A total of 25,000 women were transported, about one-sixth of all those sent.

People who had taken part in political protests were a small minority of the transported prisoners. These included radicals, Chartists, trade unionists and Irish nationalists.

What happened to the convicts?

After being sentenced:

1 **Waiting.** Prisoners were transferred to hulks – disused warships moored just off the coast of Britain. They were kept there until enough prisoners were gathered together for a voyage. Many died in the disease-ridden, unhygienic conditions (Source 1).

2 **The Voyage.** Conditions on the voyage were terrible, especially in the early years, and many died. Improvements by the 1830s reduced the deaths of convicts to only one per cent, but conditions were still cramped and unpleasant.

3 **Arrival.** On arrival, convicts were assigned to settlers – to work for them. The masters had to provide only food, clothes and shelter. How they were treated was a matter of luck. Many owners used the convicts as slave labour (Source 2) and flogged them repeatedly, but some treated their assigned convicts well.

4 **The Ticket of Leave.** Good conduct won a 'ticket of leave' for prisoners – early release. The ticket gave prisoners a real motive for good behaviour and a sense of opportunity they had never had in Britain because they could see the chances to build a new life in Australia.

5 **Punishment for bad behaviour.** Prisoners who committed further crimes were treated extremely harshly. Flogging with the 'cat o' nine tails' was widely used, with 200 lashes a common sentence. Special penal colonies were set up, for example in Tasmania, for those who committed crimes while in Australia.

Source 2

▲ A hard labour gang of convicts working in Tasmania

Source 1

▲ Convicts being rowed out to a prison hulk

Source 3

Edward Carr, an official in Tasmania, writing in 1831

It is true the convicts are sent out here as punishment. But it is equally true that it is not in the interests of the master to make his service a punishment but rather to make the condition of the convict as comfortable as he can afford. The interests of the master contradicts the object of transportation [punishment].

Source 4

A letter dictated by Richard Dillingham to his parents. Dillingham had been sentenced for taking part in protests in 1830–1831. He was assigned as a gardener to the colony's architect, a kind and considerate man.

As to my living I find it better than I ever expected thank God. I want for nothing in that respect. As for tea and sugar I could almost swim in it. I am allowed a pound of sugar and quarter of a pound of tea per week and plenty of tobacco and good white bread and sometimes beef sometimes mutton sometimes pork. This I have every day. Plenty of fruit puddings in the season of all sorts and I have two suits of clothes a year and three pairs of shoes a year. I want for nothing but my liberty but it is not the same with all that come as prisoners.

Activity

Step 2: Consider whether transportation is still achieving its aims

Fill out your own copy of this table using the information on pages 92–95, including the notes provided below.

Aim of transportation	Is transportation achieving this aim? (Give evidence to support your judgement)
An alternative to hanging	
A deterrent	
To get rid of criminals	
To reform criminals	
To allow Australia to be settled and developed	

Many ex-convicts have reformed and now live peacefully and find work in Australia.

Transportation costs £0.5 million per year. There are more prisons in Britain now and they cost less money than transportation.

The free settlers in Australia have set up societies to protest against us 'dumping' convicts in their country.

Crime has not fallen in Britain since transportation to Australia began.

Australia is now well established as a secure part of the British Empire. No other country is likely to try to claim control of Australia.

Transportation is now seen as more of an opportunity than a punishment by many people in Britain. Lord Ellenborough said in 1810 that transportation was, 'No more than a summer's excursion to a happier and better climate.'

Wages are higher in Australia than in Britain once a prisoner has won their ticket of leave.

In 1851 gold was discovered in Australia. A gold rush began with thousands of people in Britain trying to find the money to buy a ticket to Australia.

Step 3: Make your proposal

Use the information in your table to make a proposal to your Minister as to whether transportation should be abandoned. You will need to consider whether it:

a was a success

b is still needed.

When was the best time to be in prison?

Britain changed very quickly during the years 1750–1900, and the country struggled to cope with the changes. Given the crime wave shown in Source 3, page 86, it is not surprising that one of the issues people debated most was punishment. It took a while to realise that more crime meant that more prisons were needed. But, having decided that more prisons had to be built, the country used some of its massive wealth for a huge prison-building programme – 90 prisons were built between 1842 and 1877. But that was only the beginning. What should these prisons be like? What was the purpose of prison? Britain went through not just one, but a number of prison revolutions.

So what was it like to spend time in prison during these years?

Activity

For this task imagine you are a convict serving five years in prison.

Use a table like this one to record your judgements about which of the four types of prison you would rather find yourself in to serve out your five year stretch. (Remember that 'good' and 'bad' in columns 2 and 3 are from the convict's point of view.)

Period and style of prison	What was good about it?	What was bad about it?
1 An old, unreformed prison, about 1810		
2 After the first reforms, about 1830		
3 Under the Separate System, about 1850		
4 Under the Silent System, about 1870		

1 The old prisons

In the early 19th century, most prisons were much the same as they had been for centuries. In fact, in some places the local prison was still the dungeon of the medieval castle! You know about these from reading about the work of Elizabeth Fry and John Howard. You can look back to pages 88–90 to remind yourself what these were like, but here are the key features:

- All prisoners were housed in together: first offenders, old lags (habitual convicts), debtors, lunatics, women, children.

- Jails were often dirty, damp, overcrowded and unhealthy. What was called 'gaol fever' (probably dysentery or typhus) killed many inmates.

- Jailers were not paid, so they made their money by charging prisoners. If you were well off you could have your own cell, good food, beer, tobacco, visitors – even keep a pet; if you were poor, your life was grim. You had to pay a fee to be released.

Source 1

Fees payable to the jailer at Newgate prison, 1729

Admission fee: 3 shillings

A shared bed: 1 shilling and three pence a week

Your own bed: 2 shillings and 6 pence a week

Release fee: 6 shillings and 10 pence (Six shillings and 10 pence was about three days' wages in 1729.)

2 After the first reforms, 1820s

Following the work of Elizabeth Fry, John Howard and others, the government eventually began to address the problems in prisons.

Home Secretary Robert Peel's Gaols Act (1823) only applied to the biggest prisons – about 130 – in London and in the larger towns and cities. The Act said:

- Prisons had to be healthy, with proper fresh water supply and drains.
- Prisoners were not allowed to keep pets, but were to have enough proper food.
- Jailers had to be paid.
- Each prison was to have a paid Governor, and a chaplain. Prisoners had to attend chapel and receive religious instruction.
- Prisoners had to be separated into different groups. Women had to be looked after in separate women's sections, with female warders.
- Warders wore a uniform.
- Magistrates had to visit prisons in their area and check on them.

Note: this Act was often ignored, but it did have some impact.

Governments were beginning to realise that they had to do something and the first new prisons were built. Millbank Prison was opened in 1816 and cost £450,000 (£20 million in today's money). The new prisons were built in a completely new style (see Source 2).

Children in prison

The move towards treating young offenders differently and housing children in separate institutions rather than in an adult prison took a long time.

- In 1838 Parkhurst Prison was opened, the first prison solely for the young. Prisoners spent four months in solitary confinement except for silent exercise, chapel services and lessons. Then two years were spent in leg irons.
- In 1870 the Education Act made education compulsory for children aged five to ten for the first time. Later Acts extended compulsory education to older children. This had the greatest impact on reducing juvenile crime because children were no longer on the streets in daytime.
- In 1899 children were at last no longer to be sent to prisons with adults. Instead, special reformatory prisons were set up called borstals, after the Kent village of Borstal where the first one opened in 1902 (see pages 126–127).

Source 2

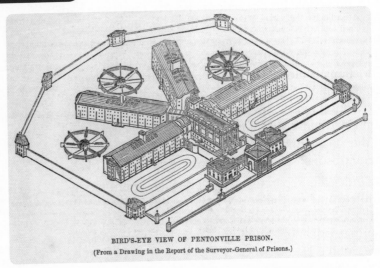

BIRD'S-EYE VIEW OF PENTONVILLE PRISON.
(From a Drawing in the Report of the Surveyor-General of Prisons.)

▲ This purpose-built prison is solid, secure, with quite large cells – 4.5m x 3.5m, each with a washbasin and barred window. The design, like spokes around a wheel hub, gave warders a clear view of a whole wing of the prison from the central area.

These prisons are still the basis of Britain's prison system today, although now with two or even three prisoners in cells designed for one.

Source 3

▲ A teenage boy photographed while serving a sentence in Bedford prison, around 1870

3 Under the Separate System

Why do people become criminals? Are they born bad? Or do their lives, their friends, their circumstances, turn them to crime? Victorians debated long and hard about these issues. It was a deeply religious time: Christians could not believe that human beings were totally evil. If only they could get a criminal away from wicked influences, make him face up to himself, give him Christian instruction, then he would be reformed. In the 1840s, this belief led to the Separate System in many prisons, such as Pentonville – opened in 1842.

Under the Separate System prisoners spent nearly all their time on their own, in their cells. It was extended solitary confinement. Even when they took exercise, prisoners could not see or talk to anyone else (see Source 1).

Religious instruction was very important, but even in the chapel prisoners were not supposed to see or communicate with one another (see Source 2).

Source 1

▲ Prisoners at exercise under the Separate System. Each is wearing a face mask with a long, low peak, and holds a rope with knots at 4.5m intervals.

Source 2

▲ This prison chapel has been specially constructed so that each prisoner is boxed in, only able to see the preacher and the guards.

Source 3

A prison chaplain describes the impact of the Separate System

A few months in the solitary cell renders the prisoner strangely impressionable. The chaplain can then make the brawny navvy cry like a child; he can work on his feelings in almost any way he pleases.

It is surely not surprising that many prisoners broke down. Extended solitary confinement is now banned. In the first eight years at Pentonville, which used the Separate System, 22 prisoners became insane, 26 had nervous breakdowns and 3 committed suicide.

4 Under the Silent System

By the 1860s times were changing again. Few people were being hanged and transportation had stopped in 1857. Prison had become the main form of punishment for more serious offences. Although the crime rate was actually falling slowly, public opinion was swinging away from reform, towards the view that there was a 'criminal class'. These 'criminal types' could never be reformed, they could only be deterred from committing more crime by harsh punishments and a tough regime in prisons. This was the Silent System.

Anyone committing a second offence received a minimum of five years' prison with hard labour. For the first nine months they were locked in their cells and after that the regime was: 'Hard labour, Hard fare, Hard board'.

Source 4

▲ The treadmill

Activity

So when was the best time to be a prisoner? Use your findings and the table on page 96 to make your decision.

smarter revision tip

You could make **revision cards** to help you to revise an important topic like changes in prisons and punishment. See pages 32–33 to remind yourself of how to make revision cards.

Hard labour

Gone were any reforming ideas of 'useful work' or learning a trade. Hard labour was tough and deliberately pointless. In some prisons, prisoners walked the treadmill (see Source 4) for several hours every day. In others, they had to turn a weighted crank in their cell (see Source 5). There was a counter so the warder could see how much work the prisoner had done: 1,800 turns to 'earn' a breakfast; 4,500 for dinner, and so on. Some prisoners did oakum-picking – separating the fibres from old ships' ropes so that it could be re-used.

Hard fare

Food was adequate, but monotonous, with the same menu every day, year in year out.

Hard board

Hard bunks replaced hammocks.

All this was to be done in silence. Any breaking of the silence rule would be punished by flogging, or being put on a diet of bread and water.

The 1865 Prisons Act appointed a new Director of Prisons, Sir Edmund du Cane, who enforced the Silent System.

The 1877 Prisons Act finally took all prisons out of local control and put them under the Home Office. The Home Office is still in control of prisons today.

Source 5

▲ The crank. Prisoners had to turn this wheel a certain number of times to earn their next meal.

On the last four pages you saw how prisons changed in the 19th century – several times. One way of understanding these changes is to see them as a pendulum swinging from one side to the other.

The purpose of prison is to show that society disapproves of what someone has done. It also prevents that person from being able to commit more crimes for as long as they are locked up. But what **should** prisons be like?

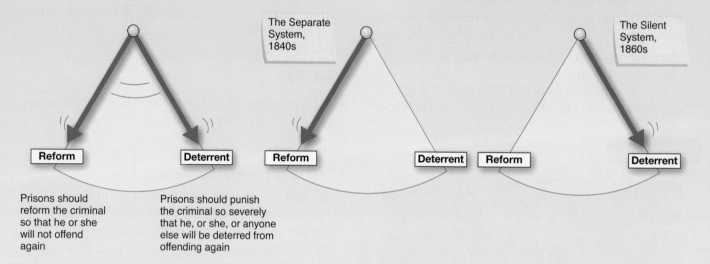

The Separate System, 1840s

The Silent System, 1860s

Reform | Deterrent | Reform | Deterrent | Reform | Deterrent

Prisons should reform the criminal so that he or she will not offend again

Prisons should punish the criminal so severely that he, or she, or anyone else will be deterred from offending again

Using the pendulum

In the case of prisons, you will find the punishment pendulum swings backwards and forwards throughout the last 200 years, as governments and the public change their minds about what prisons should be like.

1 Do you think we have marked the two systems above correctly on the pendulum?

2 What evidence about the two systems would you use to support your decision? On a copy of the pendulum, position one arrow for the Separate System and another for the Silent System. Then list the evidence to support your decision.

3 Decide where the arrow should point for each of these prison regimes:
- the old prisons, up to the 1820s – see page 96
- reformed prisons after 1823 – see page 97
- 20th century prisons – see pages 124–125
- prisons today – see page 125.

For each regime, position an arrow on a copy of the pendulum and list the evidence for your decision.

4 You could use the pendulum to analyse other forms of punishment in different periods. Make a large wall chart timeline like the one below. Think about where to draw the arrow on each pendulum.

5 Alternatively, you could use an IT spreadsheet to create your own timeline, with notes.

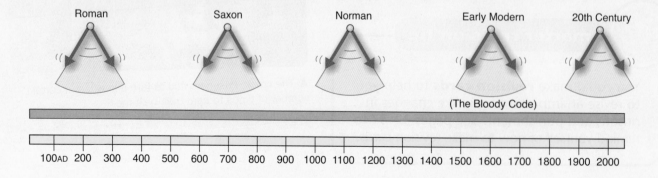

Roman   Saxon   Norman   Early Modern   20th Century

(The Bloody Code)

100AD 200 300 400 500 600 700 800 900 1000 1100 1200 1300 1400 1500 1600 1700 1800 1900 2000

> Study Source A. Are you surprised by this diet sheet for prisoners from 1851? Use the source and your own knowledge to explain your answer. **[9]**

Source A

Diet for prisoners serving sentences with hard labour at Bedford Prison, 1851

	Breakfast	Dinner	Supper
Sunday	1 pint (570ml) oatmeal gruel, 6oz (17g) bread	1 pint soup, 8oz (227g) bread	1 pint oatmeal gruel, 6oz bread
Monday	ditto	8oz bread, 1lb (450g) potatoes	ditto
Tuesday	ditto	3oz (85g) cooked meat, 8oz bread, 8oz potatoes	ditto
Wednesday	ditto	8oz bread, 1lb potatoes	ditto
Thursday	ditto	1 pint soup, 8oz bread	ditto
Friday	ditto	8oz bread, 1lb potatoes	ditto
Saturday	ditto	3oz cooked meat, 8oz bread, 8oz potatoes	ditto

---

The target for this kind of question is: 'Using sources effectively and **placing them in context**'. You will only be surprised – or not – if what the source tells you doesn't fit into what you know of the context. What was the situation at the time the source was produced?

There are two stages to answering this type of question:

First, you have to work out what the source is about, making inferences as well. Making an inference means 'reading between the lines'. Source A seems very factual: it is simply a list of how much of what food each prisoner was supposed to receive each day of the week. But by reading between the lines there are a number of inferences you can make:

- imagine living on this diet: it is extremely boring – repetitive and predictable. One of the pleasures of a meal is the choice of food a free person can make – not for these mid-19th century prisoners. The repetitiveness was deliberate – to remind them that they were not free, and all choices and all pleasures, including small ones, had been lost

- how nutritious do you think this diet was? With meat protein only twice a week, and a small amount

at that, prisoners would barely have had the energy to do the hard labour they had been sentenced to. They must have been permanently exhausted.

Second, you have to think about the question: 'Are you surprised by ... ?' To answer this, you need to know the context of the source. Look back to what you found out about prisons in the 1850s, on pages 98–99. This diet sheet indicates the prison regime of the Silent System, or 'Hard labour, Hard fare, Hard board' – particularly the second of these. Prison was supposed to be tough – a deterrent to the 'criminal classes'. So, in this case, you would not be at all surprised.

In conclusion

Read the source carefully: do you understand it?

Read the attribution: when was it produced? Who wrote it?

What do you know about this topic that helps to put this source in its context?

Are you surprised? In other words, does the evidence from the source fit with what you know about that person or that situation?

Smarter Revision: Hunting factors

Over the last few pages you have been finding out about the dramatic changes that took place in punishment policies in Britain in the 19th century – the end of the Bloody Code, the rise and fall of transportation, changes to prisons.

Big changes in history usually have more than one cause and you've already seen how some, or all, of the nine key factors we met on pages 4–5 have affected crime and punishment in some way.

Can you hunt down the factors involved in the big changes described in this section?

Activities

Draw a table to identify the ways that each of the nine factors has led to changes in how law breakers were punished. In the first column, list the nine factors. Add three columns headed 'End of the Bloody Code', 'Transportation' and 'Prison reform'.

1 Elizabeth Fry

2 John Howard

3 Fall in number of executions

4 Rise in number of crimes

5 Need to remove criminals

6 Belief in a 'criminal type'

7 Belief that people can be rehabilitated

8 Reading sensational reports about crime in newspapers

9 1840s depression: lots of people out of work

10 John Howard's report on *The State of Prisons in England and Wales*, 1777

11 Juries reluctant to convict on minor crimes

12 Judges reluctant to pass death sentences

13 Cost of transportation

14 Value of 'useful work'

15 Children needed to be diverted from turning to a life of crime

16 Samuel Romilly

1 Take each of the 18 points in turn and decide which factors it is an example of. Add it to your table in the correct box.

2 Are there any links between factors? (Are there items which could go in more than one box?)

3 In one minute, explain to the rest of the class which factor you think had the greatest impact on changes in punishment in the 19th century.

17 Ocean-going ships to take convicts to Australia

18 Britain was richer, so governments had money to spend on prison building

> Explain the ways beliefs and ideas at the time affected the punishments set out in the Bloody Code. [7]

In this type of question you are given one of the factors affecting crime or punishment – in this case Beliefs and Ideas – and you have to find examples, from any time period. Use a Smarter Revision factor chart, described opposite, to focus your revision on the nine factors.

You need to be able to recall your examples from memory, whichever factor you get asked about.

The **command word** for this type of question is: '**Explain …** ' These are therefore causation questions: you need to show the link between the **factor** and a specific punishment in a specific time. The three answers below have used the Bloody Code as an example of punishment affected by Beliefs and Ideas.

So, what do you have to do to collect all of the marks available? When you do your revision, find at least two examples from the whole history of crime and punishment to illustrate each factor. Learn a few details about each example.

- The magic number is **two**. Give two examples.
- Explain them as fully as you can.

meet the examiner – improve that answer!

Activity

Look at the three answers below. These answers would not get many marks. How could you improve each of them?

1 *Beliefs and Ideas have had an impact on punishments throughout time. When criminals were executed this was because people believed that hanging was right because the criminal deserved it. They also wanted it to warn anyone else that they would be hanged if they did the same thing.*

The Examiner says: 1 mark only. These statements could apply to almost any time in history when executions were used.

The Examiner says: 4 marks. This is a simple explanation of the beliefs and ideas behind the Bloody Code, which is accurately dated.

2 *The Bloody Code was a list of over 200 crimes which carried the death penalty. It was brought in because the upper classes, who passed the laws, believed it would scare people off from committing these crimes.*

The Examiner says: 2 marks. This is really a description, with just a brief bit of explanation. It describes the Bloody Code, without telling us when it was in force. It describes the belief that the Code would act as a deterrent, but goes no further.

3 *The Bloody Code was a set of 200 or more offences which carried the death penalty. It was in existence from the late 17th century to the early 19th century. The Code existed because there was almost no police or law enforcement system. The ruling classes, who passed the laws, feared that people would get away with crimes unless they were deterred by really serious punishments.*

5.4 Why did it take so long for the British to accept the police?

Britain in the early 19th century was an industrialised, urbanised country but its policing system was the opposite. The system was hundreds of years old and more suited to small villages. The big industrial cities clearly needed a very different kind of policing but it took ages for people to agree what this should be. In this enquiry, you investigate *why* this took so long.

In the early 1800s, the police force was:

- **parish constables:** local people appointed for a year at a time, a system dating back to the Anglo-Saxons
- **watchmen:** set up under a law passed in the 1660s in Charles II's time, so they were called 'Charleys'. They were supposed to patrol the streets at night and had a watchman's box to rest in.

The system was designed when the population of Britain was 4–5 million and, apart from London, no town had more than 10,000 people. But by 1800 the British population was 12 million and rising fast. Several cities had populations of more than 50,000. For example, by 1830, Liverpool had a population of 250,000, policed by only 50 watchmen.

The Bow Street Runners

London led the way. It was the largest city in Europe, with three quarters of a million citizens. The main magistrates court in the heart of London was in Bow Street and from there Henry and Sir John Fielding (half-brothers) set out to deal with London's rising crime rate.

When Henry Fielding was appointed in 1748 he found himself in change of 80 constables, of whom he thought only six did their jobs properly. Sir John Fielding was Bow Street magistrate from 1754 to 1780. He was blind, but was said to be able to recognise 3,000 of London's criminals by their voices. He turned Bow Street Court into a sort of police station. He made sure his constables were efficient, trained and properly paid – they came to be called the 'Bow Street Runners' (see Source 1).

He also started a news-sheet, called the *Hue and Cry*, which published details of all crimes and convictions in the London area. It was the beginning of a national crime information network.

However, progress towards a proper police force was still slow. The River Thames Police was set up in 1798 to co-ordinate efforts against crime along the whole river; in 1805 a patrol of 54 men was set up to ride the streets and stop mounted theft, but in 1800 there were still only 68 Bow Street Runners for the whole of London. All this changed in 1829.

▲ John Townsend, a Bow Street Runner

Matthew Wood, Lord Mayor of London, describes how watchmen worked in 1815.

The beats of many watchmen are so short that they take only 5 minutes to walk them, which, done twice an hour, means that he is either fifty minutes in his box, or, what is more frequent, they meet two or three together in conversation. Frequently they are employed in shutting up shops, or going on errands, or going into public houses with prostitutes. Also, from their practice of being fixed in a certain box for many years, there is no doubt some of them receive bribes from persons who commit robberies.

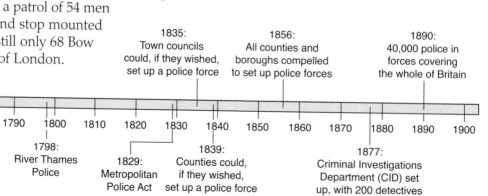

1835:
Town councils could, if they wished, set up a police force

1856:
All counties and boroughs compelled to set up police forces

1890:
40,000 police in forces covering the whole of Britain

1750 1760 1770 1780 1790 1800 1810 1820 1830 1840 1850 1860 1870 1880 1890 1900

1754:
Bow Street Runners

1798:
River Thames Police

1829:
Metropolitan Police Act

1839:
Counties could, if they wished, set up a police force

1877:
Criminal Investigations Department (CID) set up, with 200 detectives

Why was Peel able to set up the first police force in 1829?

Metropolitan Police Act, 1829

This Act set up 'The Met' – the police force for London that still goes by that nickname. A force of 3,200 police was recruited, to cover an area 7 miles (11km) around the centre of London. They became known as 'Peelers' (see Source 4).

This was a major change for London. Why did it happen?

Fear of crime

There was a widespread fear of crime and the middle and upper classes wanted it to be controlled.

Constables and watchmen couldn't do the job

The old system of constables and watchmen was looking very inadequate – see Sources 2 and 3.

> **Source 3**
>
> John Hopkins Warden, a constable in Bedford, writing in 1821 about the problems of the system of constables
>
> [A part-time parish constable] who is perhaps new to his office every year and cannot be aware of criminals' habits and plans also has his own business to take care of. He knows that his term of office as constable will soon expire so he does not give it the attention it requires.

Fear of big urban populations

The middle and upper classes feared that in the new, huge cities, especially London, the masses of people crammed into the closely packed streets, illiterate and without the right to vote, were a potential criminal threat.

Fear of revolution

After the French Revolution of the 1790s, governments and landowners in Britain feared that a similar revolution might take place in Britain. In the years after 1815 there were many protests about lack of democracy (see pages 110–111), as well as unemployment and high food prices.

Government and taxation

As you have seen in the pages on prison reform, governments were increasingly involved in changing life in Britain. Part of the reason was the long wars against France, which had forced the government to raise money. Governments were raising money through taxes and were also allowing local authorities to raise local taxes to pay for setting up a police force.

Sir Robert Peel

Peel was the Home Secretary who set up the Metropolitan Police. He had the political and administrative skills to find a solution to the problems and to win support for setting up a police force.

Source 4

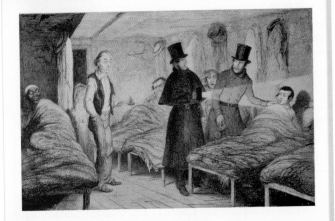

▲ 'Peelers' making an arrest, 1848

Activities

1 Was the idea of a police force for London completely new in 1829?
2 Write a one sentence summary of how each of the following contributed to setting up the Metropolitan Police:
   - fear of crime
   - fear of big urban populations
   - inadequacies of the existing system
   - fear of revolution
   - increasing government involvement.
3 Which of these best explains:
   - why pressure for a police force increased after 1815
   - why the first proper police force was set up in London?

How did attitudes to the police change?

In the beginning, there was lots of hostility towards the Metropolitan Police. Some people drove their coaches straight at policemen working on traffic control. Magistrates objected to the fact that the Metropolitan Police were not under their control, but under that of the Home Secretary. The rest of the country was slow to copy London.

One of the objections to the new police force was that they would be used as 'secret police', interfering in the liberties of citizens. Peel made every effort to prevent the new police looking like soldiers. They wore top hats, blue coats (to contrast with most soldiers' red coats) and carried truncheons rather than swords. However, they still had a military appearance, causing continued suspicion. An extreme example of anti-police feeling was in 1833 when PC Culley was killed while policing a pro-democracy demonstration. His killer was acquitted by the jury, who all received medals from a public subscription.

There was a rapid turnover of police constables in the early years. Of the initial force of 3,200, only 562 remained four years later. The worst problem was drunkenness, a common problem in the early forces, which led to 80 per cent of dismissals.

But the tide of public opinion slowly turned in their favour. By 1890 there were efficient police forces in every city, town and county in Britain. Nasty nicknames, like 'blue lobsters' or 'blue devils' disappeared in favour of the more positive 'bobby' – stemming from Sir Robert Peel's first name. From the later 19th century until the 1950s, 'the bobby on the beat' – friendly, firm but helpful, maybe not very bright but very courteous, and most importantly unarmed – was a British stereotype.

Source 5

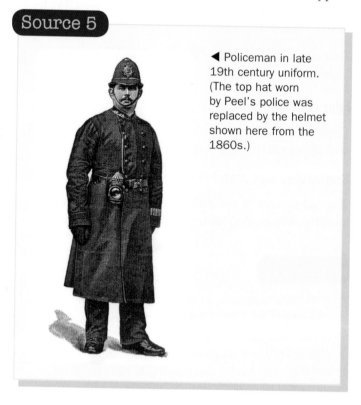

◄ Policeman in late 19th century uniform. (The top hat worn by Peel's police was replaced by the helmet shown here from the 1860s.)

Activity

Why did attitudes change?
Use the sources and information on pages 104–107 to prepare an explanation of why it took so long for the police to be accepted. You can use a table like the one below to analyse what the evidence tells you.

Source 6

The Earl of Dudley, writing in 1811 about the reaction to the Ratcliffe Highway murders, which shocked the country and led to calls for a police force.

The fact, however, I am inclined to suspect is that it is next to impossible to prevent outrages of this sort from happening. They have an admirable police in Paris but they pay for it dear enough. I had rather half a dozen people's throats should be cut in Ratcliffe Highway every three or four years than be subject to police visits to my home, spies and all the rest of the French system.

Reasons for opposition to a police force		Reasons for acceptance of a police force	
Source no.	What the evidence tells me	Source no.	What the evidence tells me
Own knowledge		Own knowledge	

Source 7

▲ A cartoon from a song sheet published in about 1830

Source 8

A letter of complaint from Harworth parish, Nottinghamshire

The parish of Harworth has paid during the last year £21 9s 2d (£21.46p) as their quota of the expenses of maintaining the County Constabulary without receiving any benefit whatsoever.

Source 9

From *Punch* magazine, 1851

The police are beginning to take that place in the affections of the people – we don't mean the cooks and housemaids alone but the people at large – that soldiers and sailors used to occupy. The blue coats – the defenders of order – are becoming the national favourites. The taking of a foreign fort seems to sink into insignificance before the taking of an unruly cabman's number. Everyone has been charmed during the Great Exhibition by the way in which this truly civil power has been effective.

[Six million tickets were sold for the Great Exhibition of 1851, held in Hyde Park. Whole villages left home to explore the wonders of the 10,000 exhibits. The Metropolitan Police gained a great deal of credit for their helpfulness to the thousands of visitors, who were strangers to London.]

Source 10

A writer in 1836

There has been a great lessening of the amount of crime committed in London since the setting up of the new police. The great organisations of criminals have been broken up and scattered in all directions.

Source 11

Copy from a leaflet printed in 1830

Peel's Police

RAW LOBSTERS

Blue Devils

Notice is hereby given,

That a subscription has been entered into to supply the PEOPLE with STAVES … which will be in readiness to be distributed whenever an unprovoked, unmanly and blood-thirsty attack be again made upon Englishmen by a force called into existence by an illegal Parliament, passing laws for their own interest and so in opposition to the Public Good.

Source 12

▼ This cartoon from *Punch* magazine, 1866, refers to the fierce riots that took place that year calling for more democratic reforms. They were controlled by the police, not the army, and several policemen, as well as demonstrators, were injured.

RUFFIANLY POLICEMAN

You have already looked at the three main types of question you have to answer in your Development Study examination:

- 'Describe' (pages 24–25)
- 'Explain' (page 42)
- 'Evaluate a statement' (pages 52–53).

> **2** Over the course of the 19th century the government introduced a completely new system of policing Britain.
>   **(a)** Briefly describe the system for catching criminals in the 18th century. [5]
>   **(b)** Explain why the 1829 Metropolitan Police Act was passed. [7]
>   **(c)** 'The main reason why it took a long time to set up an efficient police force across Britain was because people were suspicious of their powers.' Explain how far you agree with this statement. [8]

Watch the clock – stick to a time plan

This time plan gives you a **rough guide** to approaching Question 2 on Paper 1. Pupils often spend too long writing answers containing information that is not relevant to the question. It is better to spend less time writing and more time planning your approach to each question. This should ensure that your answer focuses on the question.

1 De-code and **plan** your approach to all three questions **(approx. 5 minutes)**.
Read each question a couple of times. Highlight:

- **Date boundaries** – the time period to cover.
- **Content focus** – the topic the examiner wants you to focus on.
- **Question type** – different question types require different approaches.
- **Marks available** – a guide to how much you are expected to write.

Quickly jot down a rough plan of how you intend to approach each question. This is crucial – make sure your answer is focused on the question. Each answer should be different!

2 Answer part (a) (approx. 4–5 minutes).
This carries only 5 marks – one paragraph only.

3 Answer part (b) (approx. 10 minutes).
You need to **explain why** the Act was passed – **not** describe what it did.
   There are several reasons why the Act was passed – see pages 104–105 to remind yourself. However, many of them are linked around what people saw as the new dangers from crime in London. So use connectives to tie your answer together.

4 Answer part (c) (approx. 12 minutes).
This is an iceberg question. Use the advice opposite to help you.

5 Check your work (approx. 5 minutes).
Quickly scan your work to make sure that you have expressed yourself clearly.
- Check the spelling of key historical words, names and discoveries.
- In questions (b) and (c) make sure you used paragraphs to structure your answer and that your conclusion is clear. Does it focus on the question? Is there a clear line of argument?

What is an iceberg doing in a history book? It's here to warn you of hidden dangers lurking beneath the surface of history questions. Many students read this kind of question (question 2c on page 108) and only see what they've been given: 'suspicious of their powers' – which is the tip of the iceberg – and only write about that. But big events in history usually have lots of causes. You have to find the other reasons why it took so long to set up an efficient police force – in other words the parts of the iceberg below the surface.

So always think: ICEBERG! Don't just leap for the item you've been given – look for the hidden factors!

Watch out for the hidden part of the question

Step 1: Deal with the part of the question which is above the surface.

Explain why people were suspicious of the powers of a police force; many saw a police force as a French idea. Pro-democracy protesters were suspicious because they saw the police as the government's way of crushing them.

Step 2: Find the other factors lurking beneath the surface. This is where your explanation becomes a much more historical answer.

• Some people objected to the cost of setting up a police force.

• Some people were worried about who would control the new police forces.

• Some people thought most of the new police constables were no good at their job. They pointed out that many had to be dismissed for drunkenness.

Use the table you completed on page 106 to find these other factors. Try and show how these factors link together.

Step 3: Write your conclusion.
Don't sit on the fence: reach a judgement. Was suspicion of the police powers the main reason? End with a sentence explaining why you reached this decision.

5.5 How would you commemorate Peterloo?

On 16 August 1819, 60,000 people packed into St Peter's Fields, Manchester for a political meeting. By the end of the day, eleven of them were dead and 400 injured. The event was soon known as Peterloo. What does this event mean to us today?

Source 1

▲ This engraving of events at Peterloo was made very soon after the event.

Activities

1 Look closely at Source 1. Can you find:
  a the platform and the speakers
  b the main speaker, Henry Hunt, in his famous white hat
  c pro-democracy banners (what do they say?)
  d the magistrates, in their black hats
  e one demonstrator on the platform holding up a French Revolution 'Cap of Liberty' on a pole
  f the mass of people (men? women? children?)
  g the Manchester and Salford Yeomanry (volunteer soldiers), on horseback, with drawn sabres
  h injured or fatally wounded demonstrators lying on the ground
  i nearby houses and factories?

2 Below are ten short paragraphs telling you about Peterloo. Can you put them in the right order to make a coherent account.

3 Having got the paragraphs in the correct order, answer these questions:
  a Why were the demonstrators there?
  b Why were they killed and injured?

4 Manchester City Council have decided to put a new plaque on the wall near St Peter's Fields, to commemorate Peterloo. There is only space for 45 words. What do you think it should say?

A As the men, women and children made their way to St Peter's Fields, the local magistrates waited nervously. They had heard rumours of armed men training on the moors. They feared the meeting would be the signal for a rebellion.

B The government did not punish the magistrates. Instead, Hunt was sentenced to two and half years in prison and the three other speakers for a year. There was no enquiry and further soldiers were sent to the area.

C In 1819 the reformers decided to hold a series of mass meetings in Leeds, Birmingham, London and Manchester. Henry Hunt, one of the most rousing speakers at the time, agreed to address the crowd in Manchester.

D Britain had the most modern economy in the world – and a 17th century system of government. Only one in twenty men, and no women, had the right to vote. The French Revolution of 1789 seemed a model to many British people. They wanted the right for everyone to be able to vote in elections, so governments would be responsive to their problems.

E On 16 August 1819 men, women and children marched hand in hand in their Sunday best to St Peter's Fields. They were accompanied by flags and music. Their banners demanded 'Liberty' and 'Votes for all'.

F A horn sounded and the magistrates ordered the Yeomanry to ride forward and arrest Hunt. The Yeomanry charged the crowd; then regular troops rode in to assist the Yeomanry.

G Since 1815 bread prices had been high and unemployment had risen after many soldiers returned from the wars with France.

H Finally, the government introduced the Six Acts. These were intended to stop any chances of rebellion. Public meetings of over 50 people were banned, magistrates could seize or destroy newspapers and publications that called for reform, and they were given powers to search houses for weapons.

I Over the next couple of hours the crowd assembled on St Peter's Fields. When Hunt appeared there was enthusiastic applause: flags waved, trumpets blew, and the magistrates panicked.

J During the course of the action, eleven people were killed and around 400 were injured. The events in Manchester caused great anger and newspaper reporters in the crowd criticised the magistrates for overreacting. People demanded that the government punish the magistrates.

Sometimes you are asked to compare two sources and comment on a statement based on them. Historians like to look at several sources about the same event before making a statement about it.

Look at this question:

Study Sources A and B. Do these sources prove that the soldiers were out of control at Peterloo?

Source A

An account of what happened at Peterloo by Samuel Bamford, written in 1839. Bamford was in favour of reform and spoke at the meeting. Although his speech was moderate, he was sentenced to 12 months imprisonment for inciting a riot.

'Their sabres glistened in the air and they went direct for the hustings.* As the cavalry approached the dense mass of people, the people used their utmost efforts to escape, but so closely were they pressed by the soldiers, the hustings and their own numbers, that immediate escape was impossible. Sabres were used to cut away through naked upheld hands and defenceless heads; and then chopped limbs and wound-gaping skulls were seen and groans and cries were mingled with the din of that horrid confusion.

In ten minutes the field was an open and almost deserted space. The hustings remained with a few broken flag-poles erect and a torn or gashed banner or two. Whilst over the whole field were strewn caps, bonnets, hats, shawls and shoes, trampled, torn and bloody. Several mounds of human being remained where they had fallen, crushed down and smothered. Some of these were still groaning, others with staring eyes were gasping for breath, and others would never breathe more.'

[*Hustings: the platform the speakers were standing on]

Source B

▲ A cartoon by the cartoonist Cruikshank. He was not in Manchester on the day of the demonstration but based his drawing on newspaper accounts.

You need to look at and read the sources carefully. You must to take into account the provenance: who wrote or drew it, the date, etc.

The words of the question are strong: 'Do these sources **prove** … ?' It's not just, 'Do these sources suggest that … ?' So you have to have firm views.

Approach A

Paragraph 1 – lengthy description of Source A

> Source A explains how difficult it was to get away from the cavalry because of the number of people. It says they were hemmed in between cavalry, the hustings and the rest of the crowd. It tells us about what was left ten minutes later, with discarded clothing and some dead and wounded …

Paragraph 2 – lengthy description of Source B

> Source B tells me that the soldiers were charging into the crowd with their swords drawn. Women and children are trying to get away. Some are already dead. The people look just innocent ordinary people. The cavalrymen are shown as fat and angry …

Paragraph 3 – the answer ends with a broad statement:

> The sources therefore do prove that the cavalry were out of control.

Remember to plan your answers to 'compare' questions before you start.

✗ **Do not** go through everything that Source A tells you and then everything that Source B tells you and leave it to the examiner to pick out the similarities and differences!

✓ Instead, make direct comparisons as you go through your answer.

Don't waste time describing what each source says. Approach A, below, would score very few marks. Approach B would score much better, because the candidate has focused on the question from the start, making direct comparisons between the sources.

Approach B

Paragraph 1 – similarities between the sources

> Source B suggests that the cavalry were out of control. They are seen charging into the crowd, regardless of the close-packed mass of unarmed ordinary people. Source A supports this, as Samuel Bamford explains that the people could not escape from the sabre-wielding soldiers. He writes about 'naked up-held hands and defenceless heads.'

Paragraph 2 – differences between the sources

> However, there are some differences between the sources. In Source B the cavalry seem to be charging straight into the crowd. In Source A Bamford tells us that they were heading for the hustings, as they had been ordered to do, in order to arrest the speakers. Bamford, who was there, tells about the cries of the victims and the shouts of people trying to get away.

Paragraph 3 – an overall judgement about whether the sources, together, prove that the cavalry were out of control

> Both these sources are very critical of the cavalry and the fact that eleven people died and untold numbers were injured strongly suggests that they were out of control. But these are not the best sources to base proof on. Cruikshank was not there. He caricatures the soldiers and makes sure the public are innocent-looking. Bamford was there, but was deeply involved, so would be hostile to the soldiers who were out to arrest him and his colleagues. To prove that they were out of control you would want to see some sources from more neutral observers.

5.6 The Rebecca Riots: Why did some men dress up as women and attack gates in Wales in 1839?

Peterloo was by no means the only protest in 19th century Britain. The protesters there were demonstrating because they wanted more democracy. But protests can arise for quite different reasons. Here is another case study of a protest, this time in Wales.

▲ Rebecca Rioters attacking a gate, 1839

Look closely at the cartoon, Source 1. Do these women look a bit beefy? It's not surprising if they do: they're men – Welsh farmers. But why are they attacking a gate?

Motives

The Rebecca Riots were an unusual kind of protest. The motives of the rioters were mixed. There were economic reasons (they were poor), political reasons (they wanted more rights) and social reasons (they resented the person who owned the gate). There were even religious reasons. Grievances had been building for a long time, then there was a short term 'trigger' that set off the protest.

Can you use the information boxes to explain why these farmers are attacking this gate?

POVERTY

Farmers in west Wales were poor. Farms were small – about 20 hectares – and income might be £180 a year. Typical expenditure was:

- Rent   £60
- Tithes   £9
- Wages   £50
- Rates   £2
- Tolls   £9
- TOTAL   £130

RENT

Most Welsh farmers rented their land from landowners, most of whom were English.

TOLLS

The main roads had been taken over by a turnpike trust, which collected money to spend on improving the roads by placing gates across the road and charging people to go through them. Farmers had to pass through the tollgates to get their produce to market. They also needed lime to improve their poor soil and had to pay tolls on each cartload. In 1839 a new man, an Englishman, took over the turnpike, added four more gates and put up the tolls charged at each gate.

TITHES

These went to the Church of England, but most Welsh farmers were Welsh-speaking Methodists or Baptists. After 1839 these tithes had to be paid in cash, not farm produce.

WAGES

Farmers usually employed two labourers at £25 each per year. Landless labourers were even poorer.

RATES

These included the new Poor Rate after 1834, which was used to build the new workhouse in the nearby town of Carmarthen.

The riots

One night in 1839 some farmers broke down one of the tollgates. It was re-built, and they smashed it again. Attacks on property like this were serious: you could be transported, or even hanged. That was why, to protect themselves from identification, they dressed as women and called themselves the 'daughters of Rebecca'. They took the name from a verse in the Bible:

And they blessed Rebecca, and said to her: you will be the mother of thousands, of tens of thousands; and your children will take over the gate of their enemies! (Genesis, 24, v60).

The situation in west Wales got worse: harvests were bad, prices for farm produce were low. In 1843, the 'daughters of Rebecca' turned on other targets: farmers who had more than one farm; fathers who deserted their families; anyone who the local people disapproved of. The 'Rebecca Rioters' were becoming the enforcers of community feelings. Source 2 is an example of how they worked. The magistrates, who were mainly English, could do nothing. Juries were afraid to convict accused rioters. For a while the 'daughters of Rebecca' ruled west Wales.

Law and order

The government sent 1,800 soldiers, who managed to prevent the incident threatened in Source 2. Seventy Metropolitan policemen were also sent, and were received with a lot less hostility than the soldiers.

Then seven rioters, including one of the leaders, Jac Ty-Isha, were captured. At the same time an elderly tollgate keeper was killed in an attack. Feelings turned against mob rule. Jac Ty-Isha was sentenced to transportation for twenty years. Sir Robert Peel, then Prime Minister, agreed to listen to the farmers' grievances. In the end, tolls for farmers were reduced, and so were tithes. More Welsh magistrates were appointed, although the Welsh language could not be used in law courts in Wales for another 100 years.

Source 2

This is a translation from Welsh of a notice fastened on church and chapel doors in June 1843.

If you call yourself a man, not a boy or an old dodderer, make sure you come to the 'Plough and Harrow' next Monday morning, to pay a little visit to the mayor of Carmarthen. If you are not there, don't be surprised if your house burns down one night.

Activities

Make a plan for an answer to the question: **'Poverty was the main motive for the Rebecca Riots.'** How far do you agree with this statement?

a) Write the word 'poverty'. Add underneath it factual details to support the claim that poverty was a motive for the Rebecca Riots.

b) Now think about two other motives. Write them down, leaving space underneath.

c) Add factual details to support each of these other two motives.

smarter revision tips

You could use a **memory map** to pull together all you need to know about crime and punishment in industrial Britain. See pages 20–21 to remind yourself how to construct your own memory map. The main branches could be: Crime, Policing, Punishment and Trials.

Can you think of any good **acronyms** to help you remember some of the details?

A **timeline** would help you sort out when things happened, and how everything fits together. See page 11 for how to make and use a timeline.

Use a **concept map** like the one on page 73 to find and make links between the factors causing changes in crime, punishment and policing in the industrial period.

6.1 How did the government deal with suffragette law breaking?

In the last section you looked at two case studies about how the government reacted to 19th century protests – Peterloo and the Rebecca Riots. Democratic protest continued in the 20th century as women demanded equal democratic rights. This case study looks at how women protested and how the government dealt with them.

Christabel Pankhurst describes how she was determined to get arrested in 1905.

For simply disturbing the meeting I should not be imprisoned. I must use some certain means of getting arrested. I must 'insult' the police. Even with my arms helpless, I could commit what was technically an assault, and so I found myself arrested and charged with spitting at a policeman.

The next morning we found that the long, long newspaper silence about women's suffrage was broken.

By the late 19th century the social and legal status of women was changing. From 1870, women could keep their own money when they married; they could go to university, train as a doctor, and stand and vote in local elections. But the big issue was Parliament: women still did not have the right to vote (the suffrage) in Parliamentary elections.

Women had been campaigning for this right since the 1860s. The National Union of Women's Suffrage Societies (NUWSS), known as 'Suffragists', had 500 local branches. They held meetings, sent letters, organised petitions, and tried, unsuccessfully, to win over the all-male Parliament.

In Manchester in 1903, Mrs Emmeline Pankhurst and her two daughters, Christabel and Sylvia, founded the Women's Social and Political Union (WSPU). They were soon labelled 'suffragettes' and from the start decided that they had to get more publicity for the women's suffrage movement by breaking the law. Christabel was the first to be arrested (see Source 1). She explained her actions in court by saying that she did not have to obey a law made by men for whom she had not been allowed to vote.

Activities

The suffragettes are famous for breaking the law and using violence. But their campaign went through various stages.

1 Put the eight examples of suffragette activity A–H in chronological order. When were the turning points in suffragette actions?
2 Now match the turning points in suffragette actions against the timeline of the government's response. What links can you make?
3 How did government actions affect the activities of the suffragettes?
4 'Suffragettes had broken the law so the government were right to treat them in the way they did.' How far does the information on these pages support that view?

A 1913: Suffragette campaigning grew more violent. Many acts of arson took place, including some at all-male golf clubs and one at the home of an anti-suffrage MP. The suffragettes made sure that no animals or humans were in the buildings before they burnt them down.

B 1911: Suffragettes on hunger strike in prison were forcibly fed.

C 1912: Suffragettes used increasing violence, smashing shop windows.

D 1908: 300,000 suffragettes joined a march to Hyde Park to protest and campaign for votes for women. They carried banners in the suffragette colours of green and purple.

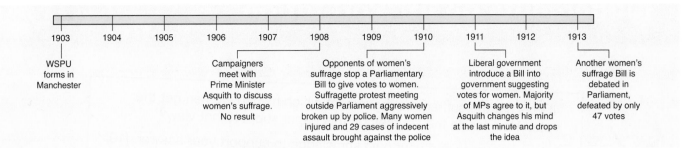

1903	1904	1905	1906	1907	1908	1909	1910	1911	1912	1913

1903 WSPU forms in Manchester

1906 Campaigners meet with Prime Minister Asquith to discuss women's suffrage. No result

1908 Opponents of women's suffrage stop a Parliamentary Bill to give votes to women. Suffragette protest meeting outside Parliament aggressively broken up by police. Many women injured and 29 cases of indecent assault brought against the police

1911 Liberal government introduce a Bill into government suggesting votes for women. Majority of MPs agree to it, but Asquith changes his mind at the last minute and drops the idea

1913 Another women's suffrage Bill is debated in Parliament, defeated by only 47 votes

How did the government respond to increasing suffragette violence?

After 1911 many suffragettes were sent to prison. To highlight their case further, many went on hunger strike. To stop women starving to death in custody, women were force fed.

Following a public outcry, the government passed a law, soon known as the 'Cat and Mouse Act' of 1913. This allowed hunger strikers to be released until they had recovered and then re-arrested and put back in prison to complete their sentence.

When the First World War broke out in 1914, women still did not have the vote.

Source 2

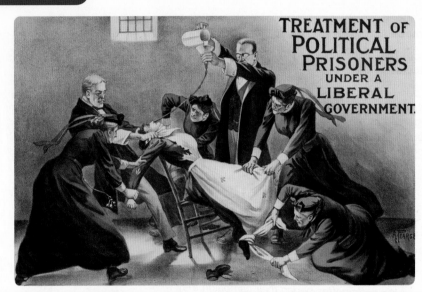

▲ This poster from the suffragette newspaper shows a woman hunger striker being force fed. The woman was held down, and a tube pushed up her nose. A milky liquid was poured into a funnel. All this was extremely painful.

E 1904: Suffragettes began to publish their own weekly newspaper called *Votes for Women*. This newspaper was sold in shops and on the streets all over the country. Women had to stand in the road as they could be arrested if they sold it on the pavement.

F 1907: Suffragettes chained themselves to railings to highlight their cause. This also meant that they had more time to protest before the police could take them away.

G 1913: At the 1913 Derby, Emily Wilding Davison wanted to highlight the suffragette case by holding up the King's horse. She was knocked down and killed. The suffragette newspaper claimed she was a martyr to the cause.

H 1908: Suffragettes were propaganda experts and sold all kinds of goods to keep their grievance in the public eye, like the teacup and saucer with the suffragette badge.

'It was not the suffragette movement which helped women get the vote.' How far do the sources on this paper support that view?

Use the sources and your own knowledge to support your answer. [10]

Source A

From *The Times*, following the death of Emily Wilding Davison in 1913

A deed of this kind is not likely to increase the popularity of any cause with the public. Reckless madness is not regarded as a qualification for the vote. There can be no doubt that yesterday's exhibition will do more harm than good to the cause of women's suffrage.

Source B

From the *Daily Mirror*, 1906

When the suffragettes began their campaign they were mistaken for featherheads, flibbertigibbets. Now that they have proved that they are in dead earnest, they have frightened the government, they have broken through the law, they have made 'Votes for Women' practical politics.

Source D

▲ A cartoon from 1906 called 'The Shrieking Sister'

Source C

Numbers of women at work, before and at the end of the First World War

	1914	1918
Munitions	212,000	947,000
Transport	18,200	117,200
Business	505,200	934,500
Farming	190,000	228,000
Industry	2,178,600	2,970,600
Domestic service	1,658,000	1,250,000
Nursing	542,000	652,000

Source E

HH Asquith, the Prime Minister, speaking in 1917 as the government prepared to give the vote to women over the age of 28.

Women cannot fight but they fill our munitions factories. They are doing work which the fighting men had to do before and this makes a special appeal to me. But what I confess moves me still more is the problem of what to do when this war is over. The question will then arise about women's work and women's role in the new order of things. I would find it impossible to withhold from women the power and the right of making their voices directly heard. Since the war began we have had no recurrence of that detestable campaign and no one can say we are giving in to violence.

Plan your approach to the question

This kind of question comes at the end of the Historical Investigation paper, which is a source-based investigation into an historical problem. This would be based on a group of six or seven sources (we are using only five here). You work your way through all the sources and are then given an interpretation which you have to comment on, using all the sources and your own knowledge.

The 'interpretation' is a little statement, cooked up by the Chief Examiner and dangled temptingly in front of you. It always sounds completely right, or completely wrong, at first reading. But beware! It's always only partly right – and partly wrong. Look at the words: '**How far** do the sources on this paper support that view?' 'How far?' already suggests that the support doesn't go all the way.

You have to review all of the sources on the paper to find the sources that support one side and those that support the other side. Then you have to reach a conclusion. You will need to spend a few minutes sketching out a **plan**. It will have three sections:

Section 1: Explore the evidence which supports the statement. Then add your own knowledge to comment on the usefulness and validity of the evidence you have found. See Example A.

Section 2: Explore the evidence which disagrees with the statement. Then use some of your own knowledge to comment on the usefulness and reliability of the evidence you have found. See Example B.

Section 3: Your conclusion. You need to reach an overall judgement: how much do you agree or disagree with the statement. Remember to explain your thinking.

Use the sources and your own knowledge!

You *must* base your answer on the sources on the exam paper. You will not achieve a good grade if you ignore the sources and simply write an answer based on your own knowledge. You do not have to use every single source but try to use most of them. Refer to the source you are using by letter so that the examiner can see which sources you are using to support your answer.

At the same time, you cannot score top marks by referring *only* to the sources. You also have to use your own knowledge of the context of the sources to comment on their usefulness and reliability.

Example A

> The cartoon, Source D, supports the statement that it was not the suffragettes' campaign that helped women to get the vote. The cartoonist calls the suffragette 'The Shrieking Sister' and has the sensible woman call the suffragette 'the cause's worst enemy'. Many men would have agreed with the cartoonist that the actions of the suffragette did not help the campaign.

> Source C shows the big part women played in the British war effort and Source E reveals how one man, the Prime Minister, who had refused to give in to the suffragettes before the war, had now changed his mind, because of women's work in making munitions. Both these sources suggest that it was not the suffragettes' campaign that helped women to get the vote.

Example B

> However, the statement is not entirely wrong. The suffragettes did raise the profile of votes for women. Source B says that they have made the issue 'practical politics'. This campaign stopped in 1914, but the issue of votes for women was not going to go away for ever – thanks to the suffragettes.

6.2 Was there anything new about 20th century crime?

The 20th century saw dramatic change in almost all aspects of the lives of the people of Britain. What about crime? Did that change too?

Changes in the 20th century

- **Standards of living** improved. People were healthier, better housed, better fed and better clothed in 2000 than they were in 1900.
- Britain was still a **divided** society, with some people very rich and many still struggling to make ends meet. However, the Welfare State was set up to give people basic security 'from the cradle to the grave'.
- Over 2.5 million British people lost their lives in the two **World Wars**; this includes over a million civilians as well as combatants.
- **New technology** perhaps had the biggest impact of all. Air travel and car ownership made everyone more mobile than ever before. Telephones, mobile phones and computers allowed people to communicate more than ever before. Cinema, radio and TV revolutionised entertainment.

The crime rate

Source 1 shows that the crime rate was low from 1870 to about 1940. The long, drawn out unemployment and poverty millions of people suffered during the 1930s Depression seems to have had no effect on the crime figures. Then came an enormous and dramatic increase in almost all kinds of crime, especially after 1960, which only began to tail off in the mid-1990s. Source 2 shows the decline in crime since then.

Has crime really increased?

In the 1980s more crime was reported and recorded than ever before. People started to report crimes like burglary because they had to for insurance purposes. It was easier to report a crime when most homes had telephones. Also, the police started to record crimes more consistently. This was partly due to policy, partly due to computer technology and partly due to changes in the law. For example, before 1977 police officers decided whether an incident of vandalism was major (defined as over £20 worth of damage) or minor (under £20 worth of damage). If it was under £20 it was not recorded in the crime statistics. In 1977 this changed and all vandalism was recorded. This meant that 150,000 more crimes appeared on the record – but had any more crime actually taken place?

Source 1

▲ This graph shows all crimes recorded by the police, 1870 to 2007. It has been adjusted to take account of the rise in population and shows the number of crimes per 100,000 people.

Source 2

British Crime Survey: 1995–2007/8

Vandalism: Down 20%	Theft from the person: Down 15%
Domestic burglary: Down 59%	Other theft of personal property: Down 53%
Vehicle-related theft: Down 66%	Drug offences: Up 61%
Other household theft: Down 53%	Violence: Down 48%
Bicycle theft: Down 34%	All crime: Down 48%

Activity

1   Source 1 shows that the amount of crime increased through the century. But has crime changed? Read page 121. Choose one example of each of the following:
   a) a new crime
   b) an old crime that looks like a new crime
   c) an old crime that got much worse

▲ One result of the 2005 London terrorist attack

Crimes against people

Murder

The number of murders increased through the century but not as fast as for other crimes. Across time, 75 per cent of murders are carried out by someone whom the victim knows and who has probably never committed a serious offence before.

Terrorism

Extreme political groups who strongly dislike the policies of the British government carried out random killings of ordinary members of the public in order to bring pressure on the government. The IRA (Irish Republican Army) carried out bomb attacks on buildings in Britain between the 1970s and 1990s, killing and injuring many people. In July 2005, Muslim extremists carried out suicide bomb attacks in London, killing 56 people and injuring hundreds more.

Violence

Crimes of violence increased, but some of this was due to changes in police practices. Until the 1990s police did not normally intervene in domestic quarrels; then they were required to do so. Police were also often lax in taking rape cases seriously but this too began to change.

> **Activity**
>
> 2 Find examples of each of these factors causing changes in crime: Government and Law Makers, Travel, Beliefs and Ideas.

Crimes against property

Car crime

There were only a few cars on the roads in 1900, but by the 1930s motoring had become popular, affordable – and deadly dangerous. Early road death tolls were extremely high: 7,343 people were killed in 1934, when there were only two million cars on the road. (In 2007, with over 30 million cars on the road, 2,940 people were killed.) The law has been heavily involved in trying to deal with this slaughter. From 1935, drivers have had to pass a driving test. They have to have insurance, tax and a roadworthy car. Once the driver has got on the road another set of laws affect speed, parking, care when driving, wearing a seat belt (since 1983) and not consuming alcohol (since 1967).

Breaking any of these laws and regulations brings car owners before the law. Even in 1939, offences involving motor vehicles made up 25 per cent of all offences. Enforcing these laws meant lots of new work for the police. Motoring offences also brought the police up against middle class law breakers.

Car theft, or theft from cars, increased the number of thefts, and now makes up half of all thefts.

Smuggling

Smuggling continued, even though the goods smuggled changed. For some years after 1945, there was a 33 per cent duty on foreign watches, so some people thought it was worth smuggling them in to Britain. By 2000, increased drug use in Britain meant that drug smuggling became lucrative and widespread. And restrictions on immigration led to a rise in people smuggling.

Theft, burglary and shoplifting

Thieves and burglars operated in much the same way as always, although they stole different things. The rise in drug addiction fuelled the rise in thefts: half of all addicts admitted to stealing to feed their habit. In the 20th century supermarkets changed the look of shops in Britain, and contributed to making shoplifting easier.

Computer crime

Computer crime is mostly theft or fraud. It can mean breaking into bank accounts and diverting money from them. It can mean hacking into confidential records and selling the information to rival companies.

6.3 What factors have caused changes in policing since 1900?

On page 106 you saw that by 1900 the 'bobby' had become a familiar and trusted part of the scene on every British street. The 20th century was a century of massive change, and the police were no exception. What factors led to these changes?

	The situation in 1900	Developments 1900–2000
Numbers and organisation	42,000 police 188 police forces	1950: 78,000 police; 120 police forces
The Police Constable	No women police 1890 Police Act: gave police a career structure, pensions Many police still unhappy about pay and restrictions, e.g. not allowed to take in lodgers, own a dog, sell vegetables from his garden	1918: Police strike, led to better pay and removal of restrictions, but a ban on striking 1920: First women police constables 1996: First woman Chief Constable
Training	No training	1947: National Police Training College at Bramshill
Communications and records	A whistle	1901: Telephone 1901: National Fingerprint Record 1910: Radio 1937: 999 call
Transport	A policeman walked his 'beat', up to 20 miles a day	1909: Bicycles 1919: Cars 1930s: Motorbikes
Special units	1798: River Thames Police 1848: Metropolitan Police had eight detectives 1877: CID (Criminal Investigation Department)	1919: The Flying Squad. Includes armed officers

The situation today

136,000 police
41 police forces

Policewomen make up 22 per cent of the force
Good pay
Some police find the job lonely

Fourteen weeks' training before starting
Specialist training during service

Instant access to computer-held records of all vehicles, missing persons, fingerprints, DNA records

Motorbikes, patrol cars, helicopters

Many specialties, e.g. Fraud Squad, Drugs Squad, Dog Handlers, Community Relations, Anti-Terrorist Squad, Scene of Crime Officers

Crime prevention: Do it yourself
For a number of reasons – the increase in crime, more valuable possessions in ordinary homes, mistrust of the police – many people and towns have set up their own new methods of crime prevention:
- neighbourhood watch
- CCTV (closed circuit television)

Activities

1 Find examples of each of these three developments causing changes in the role of the police since 1900.
   a) Changes in crime
   b) Changes in technology
   c) Changes in government policy.
2 Which of the three developments do you think has caused the greatest change to the work of the police?

Criminal moment in time 5: The 21st century
Each of the other periods you have studied included a 'Criminal moment in time' – a big picture that summed up what was going on in crime, punishment and policing. But this time you are going to devise your own 'Criminal moment in time' for the present day.

3 Look back to the other criminal moments, in Roman Canterbury (pages 12–13), in Saxon England (pages 26–27), in 18th century Portsmouth, (pages 56–57), and mid-19th century London (pages 82–83), to remind yourself what they should cover.
4 Choose a photo or sketch a picture of the place where you live. Put that in the centre of a large sheet of paper.
5 Add pictures, arrows and labels all around to explain what is happening in crime, punishment or policing. You can use what you have found out about crime and crime prevention so far in this section. And you can add your own research and local information. Here are some suggestions for what you could include in your 'Criminal moment' illustration:
- someone breaking into a car to steal it
- CCTV camera helping to catch criminals
- a car with bald tyres, or no MOT, or no insurance, or illegally parked
- someone selling smuggled tins of beer
- a 'neighbourhood watch' placard on a lamp post
- a police car speeding to the scene of a crime
- a shoplifter running out of a shop pursued by the store detective
- a group of convicted people doing community service
- someone seen through a window, at a computer, hacking into other people's bank accounts
- a house with security grilles on each window.

6.4 How did the punishment pendulum swing after 1900?

On page 100 we used the 'punishment pendulum' to analyse the changing aims of prisons in the 19th century. The pendulum continued swinging in the 20th century. Find out how and why.

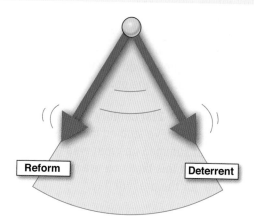

Reform | Deterrent

Changes in prison conditions

Following the adoption of the 1895 Gladstone Report, prisons moved away from the Silent System. The report set very different aims (see Source 1). Sir Edmund du Cane resigned and two reforming Prison Commissioners succeeded him: Sir Evelyn Ruggles-Brise, 1895–1921, and Sir Alexander Paterson, 1921–1947.

- 1921: Paterson ordered that ' … the close cropping of the hair of convicts should be abolished and in future the hair of all male prisoners should be cut like that of a respectable man in ordinary life.' The broad arrow uniform was abolished and replaced by more normal clothes. (See Source 2.)

- 1923: Prisoners were allowed to meet and talk to each other at certain times.

- 1936: The first 'open prison' was established at Wakefield. Open prisons had fewer restrictions, and prisoners went out to work during the day, as a preparation for leading a normal working life on release.

- 1948: The passing of the Criminal Justice Act. Flogging of prisoners was abolished. Prisoners received education and work training to help them 'go straight' when they were released. More visits from families were allowed, to keep them in contact with their communities.

Source 1

An extract from the Gladstone Report, 1895

Prison discipline should be designed to awaken prisoners' moral instincts, to train them in orderly and industrious habits, and, wherever possible, to turn them out of prison better men and women, physically and morally, than when they went in.

Source 2

Prison Commissioner Sir Alexander Paterson, 1921

You cannot train men for freedom in conditions of captivity.

Avoiding prison

At the same time, efforts were made to keep offenders out of prison.

- 1907: The Probation Service was started.
- 1967: The introduction of suspended sentences – the offender could stay out of prison if no more offences were committed.
- 1972: Community service was started. Instead of going to prison, offenders undertook many hours of unpaid work on useful projects for the community, supervised by a probation officer.

Even so, the prison population continued to rise from the 1940s onwards (see Source 3).

Activities

1 What did the Gladstone Report (Source 1) say about the purpose of prison?
2 What attitude to prisoners did the report take?
3 Put Sir Alexander Paterson's words (Source 2) into a sentence of your own.

Source 3

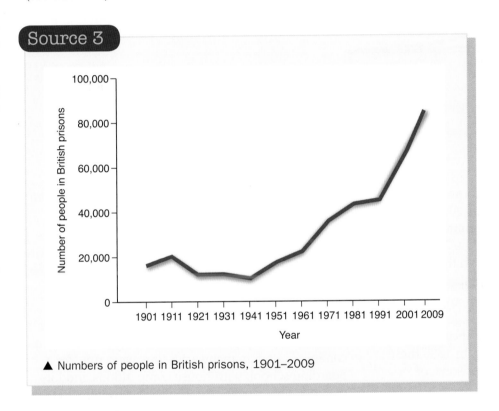

▲ Numbers of people in British prisons, 1901–2009

Prisons since the 1990s

Source 3 also makes it clear that from the 1960s the number of people in prison in Britain rose with a steep increase since the 1990s. There are a number of reasons for this:

- more crime – see Source 1 page 120
- judges giving out longer sentences
- more 'lifers':
  - the abolition of the death penalty meant more murderers serving ten years or more in prison
  - terrorists serving very long sentences – 35 years in some cases.

The increase in the prison population has brought serious problems of over-crowding. In spite of building new prisons, Britain's prisons do not have the capacity for housing the number of prisoners. This means sharing cells and fewer opportunities to work or learn a trade. In the 1990s there were serious riots at several British prisons.

Activity

4 As you saw in Section 5, at the end of the 19th century prisons were run on the deterrent principle: 'Hard labour, Hard fare, Hard board.' How did the pendulum swing in the 20th century?

Use the pendulum to analyse the approach to prison in the 20th century. Add evidence from these pages to support your decisions.

6.5 Was the treatment of young offenders in the 20th century a failure?

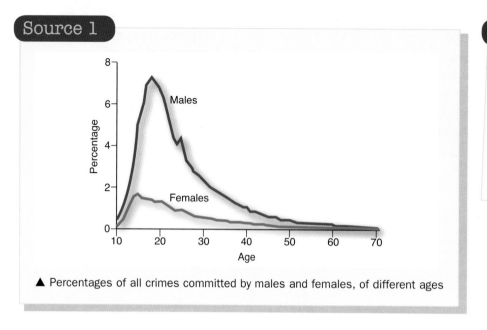

▲ Percentages of all crimes committed by males and females, of different ages

The Reverend Sydney Turner was in charge of Redhill Reformatory in the late 19th century. He believed in locking boys up alone.

… for a few days in unheated cells on a bread and water diet and whipping them with as much solemnity as possible.

Child criminals

Source 1 shows that the peak age for committing an offence, for males, is 18. For females it is even younger, 15. More than half of all crimes are committed by young males below the age of 21. Throughout the 20th century British governments struggled to deal with this situation.

Children have always committed crimes. Dickens' novel *Oliver Twist* made child crime famous, with its portrayal of a gang of child pick-pockets, led by the Artful Dodger and controlled by Fagin. If caught, they were treated no differently from adults. In 1880 there were 6,500 children under 16 in adult prisons, of whom 900 were aged under 12.

The Victorian approach to young offenders (usually called 'juvenile delinquents') was clear (see Source 2).

But we have just seen that from the early 20th century the 'punishment pendulum' was swinging towards reform. If there was one type of offender the reformers wanted to change, it was young people brought before the courts. With their characters not yet settled, it was believed that they were still open to good influences: perhaps they could be turned away from a life of crime.

Reform

The first priority was to separate young offenders from adult criminals.

- In 1908 a totally separate system of Juvenile Courts was established. They had a much less formal approach and a priority on reforming the young offender.

- In 1902 in Kent, the first borstal was opened for offenders under 18 (see page 97), and it was soon followed by others. Their purpose was to try to reform the individual by a mixture of training and care by a committed staff. In many ways they were run like a boarding school, with house competitions and lots of sport. The usual sentence was 'six months to two years': offenders could be released after six months if borstal staff thought they were ready. If not, the offender would be obliged to stay for up to two years.

In 1932, Approved Schools were started for offenders under 15. Eighty-six Approved Schools for boys were set up, and 35 for girls.

In 1948, Attendance Centres were introduced. Offenders aged 10–21 had to attend for 2–3 hours every Saturday for between 12–18 weeks. They learned basic skills – literacy and numeracy, life skills, cookery, first aid and money management. Attendees were also encouraged to make better use of leisure time. Nowadays there are victim awareness sessions, which consider the impact of offending on individuals and the community and how the young person might make amends, and sessions on drug and alcohol awareness as well as on sexual health matters.

Source 3

◀ A blacksmith's workshop at a borstal, 1945. Borstal boys were taught a trade, so they could earn an honest living when they were released.

Activities

1 Use the text below and your own timeline, 1950–2008, to plot the measures taken to deal with youth crime.

2 'The treatment of young offenders in the 20th century was a failure.' How far do you agree with this statement?

Youth detention

During the last quarter of the 20th century the tide turned against the borstal approach. Sixty per cent of young people released from borstals or Approved Schools offended again. This was taken to prove that reform was not working. There was an increase in crime, particularly youth crime, and public opinion was more interested in seeing the offenders punished. In 1982, borstals were closed and replaced by Youth Detention Centres, with fixed term sentences of between 3 and 16 weeks. These had a much tougher regime, called a 'short, sharp, shock', with lots of military drill and discipline. This policy may have pleased politicians and some newspaper headline writers, but the re-offending rate for those released was 75 per cent.

The situation in the early 21st century

Youth Courts now have a wide range of possible ways of dealing with a young offender. They work with police, social workers and probation officers and start by getting a complete picture of the young person: criminal history (if they have already offended), education, health, family, environment and attitudes. The emphasis is on preventing the young person from settling into a life of crime.

Sentences may start by binding the parents over to keep their child under control or perhaps with a fine, which the parents, of course, have to pay. If this seems unlikely to work, the child can be removed from his or her parents and put into care. Increasing concern about young people making life very difficult for their neighbours led to the introduction of measures such as ASBOs (Anti-Social Behaviour Orders) in 1999; and tagging and curfews (2003). Attendance Centres are the young offenders' last chance – a further offence will lead to them being locked up in a Young Offender Institution.

6.6 Did the abolition of capital punishment lead to more murders?

One of the stories you have been following through this course is the story of capital punishment. How did that change in the 20th century?

Throughout history the ultimate punishment has always been the death penalty. But in Britain, the number of people hanged each year had been declining since the late 18th century (see Source 2, page 85). There was a move in the 20th century away from the tough punishments of earlier periods. In 1948, the UN Declaration of Human Rights helped to change attitudes towards capital punishment. By the 1960s the number of hangings was down to about eight a year. The last woman to be hanged, Ruth Ellis, was executed in 1955.

Many Home Secretaries used their ministerial right to reprieve murderers. Minor changes were made to the procedures for hanging: for example, leaving the victim to swing for an hour after death was stopped in 1954.

Gradually the public pressure to abolish capital punishment increased. Votes on abolition were held in Parliament at various times. Each time, MPs voted to keep the death penalty, but less and less convincingly. The debate continued in the press and in Parliament.

Source 1

▲ A contemporary illustration of the execution of Dr Crippen at Pentonville prison in 1910

For and against

Those who wanted to retain capital punishment argued that:

- it had a deterrent effect
- criminals would be more likely to carry guns if there was no danger of them being hanged for killing
- life imprisonment was expensive, and in a way, even more cruel
- murderers who served a prison sentence and who would eventually be released could murder again
- it was a way of showing society's disgust and horror at crimes, for example the multiple murders of serial killers.

Abolitionists argued that:

- other countries had abolished capital punishment without a noticeable increase in crime
- mistakes were sometimes made and the wrong person executed
- most murders happen on the spur of the moment, so capital punishment is not a deterrent
- execution is barbaric and uncivilised.

Miscarriages of justice

Two well-publicised cases helped to turn the argument in favour of abolition.

Timothy Evans: hanged 9 March 1950. Timothy Evans was a van driver who, with his wife, was a lodger in the house of John Christie, at 10 Rillington Place, London. Evans' wife became pregnant and Christie offered to perform an abortion. However, Christie was a serial killer who had already murdered several women.

Source 2

▲ Supporters of Derek Bentley asking people to sign a petition against his execution

He told Evans that the abortion had been a failure and his wife had died. Evans, guilty over what had happened, confessed to murder. His story was obviously untrue, and he changed it several times but was nevertheless convicted of his wife's murder, and hanged. Three years later, Christie was convicted of other murders and it was clear that Evans had not been a murderer. He was posthumously pardoned in 1965.

Derek Bentley: hanged 28 January 1953. Derek Bentley, aged nineteen (but judged to have a mental age of ten), and Chris Craig, aged sixteen, were burgling a warehouse in London in 1952. Craig shot and killed a policeman who was trying to arrest them, but Bentley had, according to the police, shouted, 'Let him have it!' There was uncertainty over exactly what Bentley might have meant: to kill the policeman or to let him have the gun. Craig was too young to be hanged and the jury found Bentley guilty of murder, although they asked for mercy for him. Nevertheless, murder of a policeman led to powerful pressure for someone to be punished. As the Home Secretary, Sir David Maxwell Fyfe, considered whether or not to grant a reprieve, a crowd gathered outside the Houses of Parliament, chanting 'Bentley must not die!' However, their efforts were in vain and Bentley was hanged. In 1998, following a review of the case, Bentley was posthumously pardoned.

Abolition

By 1957, the death penalty applied to only five types of murder:

- murder while carrying out a theft
- murder by shooting
- murder while resisting arrest
- murder of a police officer
- a repeat murder.

Yet there was some unfairness even in the 1957 law: why was murder by shooting worse than killing by strangling or poison? The debate to abolish hanging entirely continued. The last two people to be executed in Britain were hanged in 1964. Capital punishment was abolished in 1965 for all offences except piracy and high treason in time of war. At first this was for a trial period of five years, but in 1969, on a free vote in Parliament, capital punishment was abolished by 343 votes to 185. In recent years the death penalty has been declared contrary to human rights and in 1998 it was completely removed.

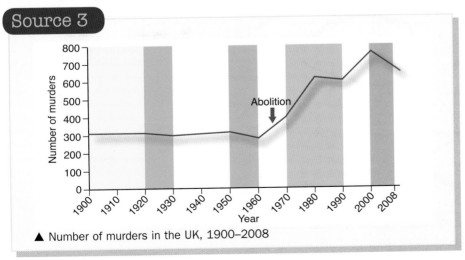

Source 3

▲ Number of murders in the UK, 1900–2008

smarter revision tips

You could use a **memory map** to pull together all you know about crime and punishment in the 20th century. See pages 20–21 to remind yourself how to construct your own memory map. The main branches could be: Crime, Policing, Punishment and Trials.

You could make **revision cards** to help you to revise an important topic like changes in punishment. See pages 32–33 to remind yourself how to make revision cards.

Use a **factor table** like the one described on page 102. Replace the items along the top with the following headings: The rise of car crime, Changes in policing, Changes in prisons; Punishment of young offenders and Abolition of capital punishment.

Throughout this book you have been introduced to a number of ways of building up information that will help you to revise. It was important to do this from the beginning so that you accumulated your information steadily throughout the course.

A word of encouragement

There probably seems a lot to learn. The amazing thing about these Smarter Revision tools is that you will find that you have already learned a lot just by looking at your notes, maps, cards, etc. and choosing what to put on each!

Just do a bit of 'Look – cover – say – write' and you'll be fine. (Don't know what that is? Ask your teacher!)

smarter revision

Let's look at all these Smarter Revision tools again, but this time, think how you could use each idea for another topic in the course.

Memory map

You were introduced to memory maps when you were studying crime and punishment in Roman times.

A memory map records the key features of crime and punishment in each period of history. It's very good at making clear the difference between BIG IDEAS and little supporting items. Our course has five periods. It would help your revision to record the BIG IDEAS for every period on five memory maps, adding in some supporting detail in each case.

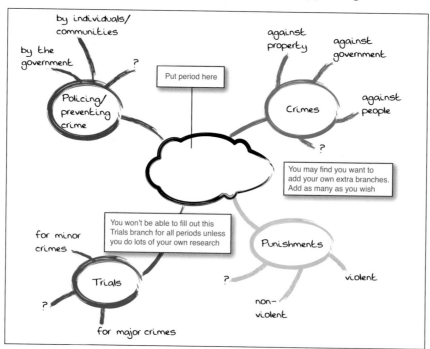

Revision cards

When you were studying crime and punishment in the Middle Ages you used revision cards to record key events in the Saxon period and to play the 'What? and Why?' game. Then you used revision cards to look at change in the Norman period.

Name of the trial	Name of the punishment	Tithing	Hue and cry
Description	Description	Description	Description
Explanation	Explanation	Explanation	Explanation
Changes	Changes	Changes	Changes

Other examples of topics which would be easier to revise if you used some revision cards are: the Bloody Code, transportation, 19th century police reform and 19th century prison reform, as well as the key changes in the 20th century.

Concept map

This kind of Smarter Revision is perhaps the most important of all. So important that we are going to look at it in more detail on the following pages. You were introduced to concept maps when you looked at the factors affecting crime in the Early Modern Period (see pages 72–73).

Concept maps look at the way that all the key factors: Government and Law Makers, Religion, Beliefs and Ideas, Key Individuals, Poverty and Wealth, Media, Taxes, Travel, and Towns, affect crime and punishment. The same nine factors have their effects in every period. It would be a very useful revision idea to see how these factors affected each of your five periods. Another way is to take each factor, and see how it affected crime and punishment right across the 2,000 years of your course.

Punishment pendulum

Is there progress in the three stories of change in crime, punishment and policing? To answer that, you need to define progress. But, as you saw on pages 100 and 124, as far as punishment is concerned, the pendulum swings between putting the emphasis on punishment, or on reforming the criminal.

Does the pendulum swing throughout history?

Timelines

Timelines are always useful and can help you to remember the chronology of periods, events and people.

Factor wheel

You have been building up your factor chart through the course. We summarise that on the next four pages.

Section 7: Conclusion: How have the factors affected change in crime and punishment?

While you have been studying crime and punishment you will have noticed that a number of 'factors' that affect change have cropped up again and again. Our task in history is not just to list or describe events from the past, but also to explain why they happened. These factors help us with those explanations.

You might have noticed that two factors in particular stand out as the most important factors that bring change in almost every period: Government and Law Makers and Beliefs and Ideas.

Government and Law Makers

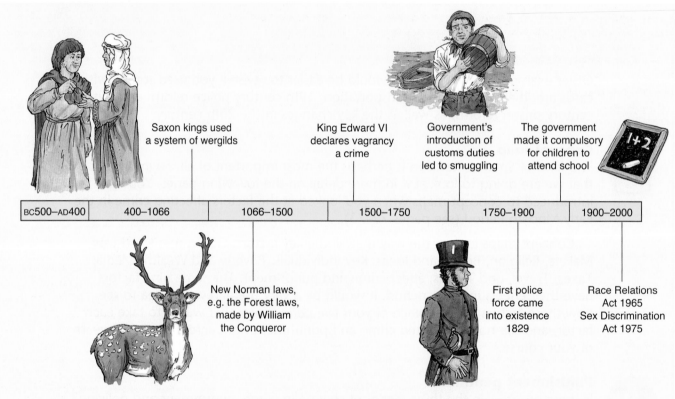

Saxon kings used a system of wergilds

King Edward VI declares vagrancy a crime

Government's introduction of customs duties led to smuggling

The government made it compulsory for children to attend school

| BC500–AD400 | 400–1066 | 1066–1500 | 1500–1750 | 1750–1900 | 1900–2000 |

New Norman laws, e.g. the Forest laws, made by William the Conqueror

First police force came into existence 1829

Race Relations Act 1965
Sex Discrimination Act 1975

Governments decide what is a crime. Governments set the punishments. Governments enforce the law.

Activity

1 From your own knowledge and using sources from this book, fill out a table like the one below with examples from each period.

Governments of the time:	Deciding what is a crime	Setting the punishments	Enforcing the law
Saxon			
Late Middle Ages			
Early Modern Period			
Industrial Britain			
20th century			

Beliefs and Ideas

The other huge influence on crime and punishment throughout history has been the impact of attitudes and beliefs. Examples can be seen on the timeline below.

Notice that two examples appear on both timelines: the Race Relations Act and the Sex Discrimination Act. These are good examples of two factors – beliefs and government – working together.

By the 1960s, Britain was becoming a more multi-racial society and racial minority groups were being discriminated against in many ways. Many people, including religious groups, believed that this was wrong. They influenced the government to introduce the Race Relations Act and make racial discrimination illegal.

In a similar way, British attitudes towards equality for women, especially in employment, were changing fast. The government reacted to these changes in attitude by introducing the Sex Discrimination Act.

So two factors worked together to change the law and once a law is changed, new crimes are created. As you revise the whole course, look for other examples of one factor working together with another or several other factors.

Activities

2 The drawings on the timeline below are examples of attitudes and beliefs that influence crime and punishment. Explain what each one shows.

3 Use this book and your studies to find other examples of attitudes and beliefs that have influenced crime and punishment. Add them to your own copy of the timeline.

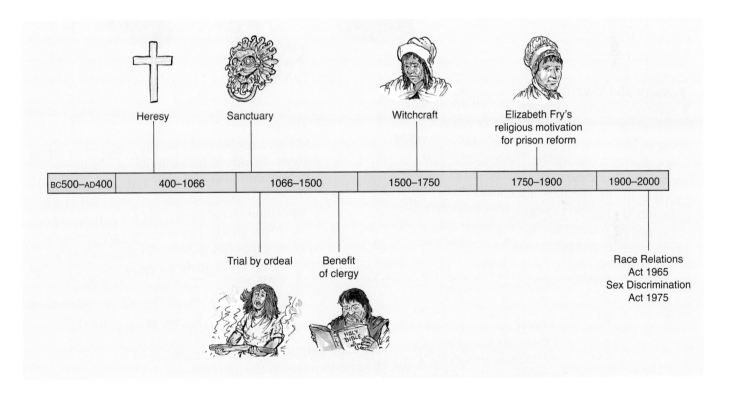

133

Other factors

Activities

1 Make your own copy of the factor wheel.
2 Use the information on Government and Law Makers and Beliefs and Ideas from earlier in this book, as well as the information on pages 134–135 to explain the importance of each factor.
3 For each factor, give one example from this book of how it influenced **crime**.
4 Find some examples of **crime** being influenced by more than one factor. Add lines between the factors on your wheel to show how factors work together.

Poverty and Wealth

1

Crime often increases when poverty increases. But the connection between the two is not simple. Not everyone who is poor turns to crime – for example, during the 1930s Depression crime didn't increase very much. Other factors, such as the personality of the individual, or the likelihood of getting caught, play their part. It may not be poverty itself, but greater inequality between rich and poor, which causes crime.

Towns

2

Crime rates have always been higher in urban areas, including, for example, in Ancient Rome. In Section 5 you saw how 19th century cities expanded very quickly. They provided plenty of opportunities for crime, and for getting rid of the stolen goods. The 19th century system of policing was based on life in villages and was hopelessly inadequate for cities.

Travel

3

People on the move can become easy victims of crime. For example, as you saw in Section 4, the increase in travel in the 18th century presented opportunities for highwaymen to operate. In the railway age, as described in Section 5, criminals could be hundreds of miles away from the scene of their crime within a few hours.

On the other hand, better means of communication help catch criminals. The murderer Dr Crippen was caught using a telegraphed message to the captain of the ship on which he was escaping to the USA. Modern policing relies heavily on rapid communications, as we saw in Section 6.

Taxes

The cost of punishment has always been important. Throughout history, prisons were regarded as too expensive until, in 19th century Britain, greater national wealth meant that the country could afford to build prisons. Transportation was ended partly because it was becoming too expensive. Governments today are looking for cheaper alternatives to prison.

4

Media

The mass media – newspapers, radio, TV – have always been interested in reporting crimes. They have sometimes sensationalised crime and given the impression that there was more crime being committed than there actually was and this can lead to a public demand for more harsh punishments. On the other hand, media campaigns about miscarriages of justice helped to bring about the abolition of capital punishment.

5

Religion

Religious beliefs had a big impact on 19th century prison reform. For example, the Silent System (page 99) was based on a belief that prisoners needed to study themselves and their religion in order to reform. On the other hand, Elizabeth Fry (pages 88–89) carried on her work in Newgate Gaol sustained by her religious belief that everyone deserved decent treatment because there was 'that of God' in everyone.

6

Key Individuals

The work of prison reformers like John Howard and Elizabeth Fry – together with other factors – changed conditions in prisons and the treatment of prisoners.

7

Activities

5 Make another copy of the factor wheel.

6 For each factor, give one example from this book of how it influenced **punishment**.

7 Find some examples of **punishment** being influenced by more than one factor. Add lines between the factors on your wheel to show how factors work together.

Index

Acknowledgements

Every effort has been made to trace all copyright holders, but if any have been inadvertently overlooked the Publishers will be pleased to make the necessary arrangements at the first opportunity.

Photo credits

Punishments handed down by Durham Assizes (see page 84)

JANE SCOTT 'To be whipped'

ROBERT BELL 'Death'.

JOHN HALL 'To be whipped'.

JOHN DIDSBURY 'Seven Years Transportation'.

WILLIAM STONEHOUSE 'To be whipped'.

THOMAS HAY 'To be whipped'.

EDWARD PERKIN 'Death'.

JOHN REED 'Death'.

JOHN SUTCLIFFE 'Seven Years Transportation'.